CHINESE
STORIES
FOR LANGUAGE LEARNERS

读成语故事，学中国历史文化

CHINESE STORIES

FOR LANGUAGE LEARNERS

A Treasury of Proverbs and Folktales in Chinese and English

Vivian Ling & Wang Peng
Illustrated by Yang Xi

TUTTLE Publishing
Tokyo | Rutland, Vermont | Singapore

"Books to Span the East and West"

Tuttle Publishing was founded in 1832 in the small New England town of Rutland, Vermont [USA]. Our core values remain as strong today as they were then—to publish best-in-class books which bring people together one page at a time. In 1948, we established a publishing outpost in Japan—and Tuttle is now a leader in publishing English-language books about the arts, languages and cultures of Asia. The world has become a much smaller place today and Asia's economic and cultural influence has grown. Yet the need for meaningful dialogue and information about this diverse region has never been greater. Over the past seven decades, Tuttle has published thousands of books on subjects ranging from martial arts and paper crafts to language learning and literature—and our talented authors, illustrators, designers and photographers have won many prestigious awards. We welcome you to explore the wealth of information available on Asia at www.tuttlepublishing.com.

Published by Tuttle Publishing, an imprint of Periplus Editions (HK) Ltd.

www.tuttlepublishing.com

Copyright © 2020 by Vivian Ling and Wang Peng

Cover image & frontispiece © Cleveland Museum of Art

Library of Congress Cataloging-in-Publication Data is in progress

ISBN 978-0-8048-5278-4

First edition
27 26 25 24 23   8 7 6 5 4   2307VP
Printed in Malaysia

Distributed by

North America, Latin America & Europe
Tuttle Publishing, 364 Innovation Drive
North Clarendon, VT 05759-9436 U.S.A.
Tel: 1 (802) 773-8930 Fax: 1 (802) 773-6993
info@tuttlepublishing.com
www.tuttlepublishing.com

Japan
Tuttle Publishing, Yaekari Building 3rd Floor
5-4-12 Osaki Shinagawa-ku, Tokyo 141 0032
Tel: (81) 3 5437-0171 Fax: (81) 3 5437-0755
sales@tuttle.co.jp
www.tuttle.co.jp

Asia Pacific
Berkeley Books Pte. Ltd.
3 Kallang Sector #04-01, Singapore 349278
Tel: (65) 6741-2178 Fax: (65) 6741-2179
inquiries@periplus.com.sg
www.tuttlepublishing.com

TUTTLE PUBLISHING® is a registered trademark of Tuttle Publishing, a division of Periplus Editions (HK) Ltd.

Contents

Why We Wrote This Book

The primary aim of this book is to provide an entertaining way for readers to learn about Chinese wit and wisdom. Our vehicle is a collection of traditional stories and the idiomatic expressions associated with them. Proverbs and idioms exist in every culture, but their prominence in Chinese culture is exceptional. The Chinese people's high regard for lessons from history, reinforced by many enduring classical references to them in everyday speech, has sustained the vitality of these stories and their idioms through the ages down to the present day.

Native Chinese readers will have a feeling of déjà vu as they read the stories in this volume and even some non-native speakers may also be familiar with a few of them. But in presenting these stories, we have used a contemporary perspective which we hope readers will find refreshing. To highlight the relevance of these traditional stories for modern readers from all cultures, we have selected ones that embody universal wisdom. Each chapter also presents a true modern story which exemplifies how the proverb or idiom applies to life in our contemporary world.

Another distinguishing feature of this collection is that we have enriched the meaning of the stories by placing them in their historical and literary contexts. In effect, each story becomes a window onto Chinese culture, history and literature. To give readers a glimpse of the treasure trove of writings from which the stories are derived, we have compiled a bibliography called "The Literary Origins of the Stories in this Book," which follows this introduction

Each story is accompanied by a set of discussion questions designed to stimulate further thoughts about the contemporary relevance of the proverbs and idioms. These questions may also serve as prompts for language students to practice their oral discussion skills.

The title of this book, *Chinese Stories for Language Learners*, suggests that it is intended mainly for students of Chinese language. In reality, the format of this book is designed to be reader-friendly to English readers as well as Chinese language students at varying levels of proficiency. For the convenience of language learners, the chapters are ordered by language level, from intermediate to high. The glossaries are pitched at the high-intermediate level. Words in the Chinese texts that are included in the glossary are underlined; those that appear in footnotes are listed at the end of the corresponding glossaries. If you find your vocabulary to be below the threshold of the glossaries, the bilingual format with English and Chinese versions on facing pages should assist you in reading the Chinese version. To minimize frustration and maximize enjoyment, we suggest that you read through the story in English first, then read it in Chinese. This will allow you to make intelligent guesses for unfamiliar Chinese vocabulary.

For intermediate and advanced students, a special benefit of this book is the acquisition of proverbs and idioms, called 成语 chéngyǔ (set phrases) in Chinese. These phrases constitute a rich feature of the Chinese language. The speech of any well-educated native Chinese person tends to be liberally spiced with them. It's easy for students at the intermediate and advanced level to fall in love with chéngyǔ, for they are eloquent, humorous and utterly unforgettable once you have learned them. Imagine yourself impressing your Chinese friends by coming up with the perfect set phrase at just the right moment!

To all readers of this little volume, we hope you will be entertained while being enlightened!

—**Vivian Ling & Wang Peng**

The Literary Origins of the Stories in this Book

The traditional stories in this book and the sayings associated with them remain very much alive in Chinese culture and language today. This reflects the Chinese people's timeless appreciation for the wisdom embedded in these stories. The original sources for the stories in this collection are some of the best-known classical works of Chinese philosophy, history and literature going back as far as the 5th century BCE. One of the aims of this book is to provide glimpses of the vast body of literature from which these gems of Chinese wisdom are derived. The list below is organized by types of works, with a chronological listing within each category. The sayings derived from each work are listed below that work. Most of the classics of philosophy were compiled by followers of specific schools of thought that bear the names of leading philosophers and are therefore not attributed to specific authors. The details of the origin of each saying in this book are given within each chapter. To minimize duplication, only the essentials are provided in the following bibliography.

1. Classical philosophical works

■ 《论语》 *The Analects of Confucius* (5th century BCE)
有教无类　With education, there is no class distinction
举一反三　Raise one example, respond with three

■ 《庄子》 *The Book of Zhuangzi* (4th–3rd century BCE)
邯郸学步　Learning the Handan walk
井底之蛙　A frog at the bottom of a well

■ 《孟子》 *The Book of Mencius* (ca. 300 BCE)
拔苗助长　Pulling up sprouts to help them grow
鱼与熊掌, 不可兼得　One cannot have both fish and bear paws

■ 《荀子》 *The Book of Xunzi* (3rd century BCE)
青出于蓝, 而胜于蓝
Azure blue is from indigo but surpasses indigo

- 《韩非子》• 韩非 *The Book of Han Feizi*, by Han Feizi (280–233 BCE)
  守株待兔　Waiting for rabbits by a tree stump
  滥竽充数　An imposter in the orchestra
- 《吕氏春秋》 *The Annals of Lü* (ca. 239 BCE)
  掩耳盗铃　Covering one's ears to steal a bell
  刻舟求剑　Marking the boat to locate a lost sword
- 《淮南子》 *The Book of Huainanzi* (2nd century BCE)
  塞翁失马，焉知非福　The old frontiersman loses a horse, how would we know that it's not a fortune in disguise?

2. Works of history

- 《战国策》 *Stratagems of the Warring States* (1st century BCE)
  狐假虎威　The fox who uses the tiger's prowess
- 《三国志》• 陈寿 *Records of the Three Kingdoms*, compiled by Chen Shou (233–297 CE)
  士别三日，刮目相看　A scholar who has been away for three days should be viewed with a fresh pair of eyes
- 《后汉书》• 范晔 *History of the Latter Han Dynasty*, by Fan Ye (398–445 CE)
  水至清则无鱼，人至察则无徒　Pure water has no fish; scrupulous people have no friends
- 《魏书》• 魏收 *History of the Wei Dynasty*, by Wei Shou (506–572 CE)
  青出于蓝，而胜于蓝　Azure blue is from indigo but surpasses indigo

3. Works of literature

- 《三国演义》• 罗贯中 *Romance of the Three Kingdoms*, by Luo Guanzhong (ca. 1330–1400 CE)
  谋事在人，成事在天　Planning lies with man but success lies with Heaven

- 《东周列国志》• 冯梦龙 *Annals of the Kingdoms in the Eastern Zhou Dynasty*, by Feng Menglong (1574–1646 CE)
  老马识途　Old horses know the way

- 《醒世恒言》• 冯梦龙 *Stories to Awaken the World*, by Feng Menglong (1574–1646 CE)
  人不可貌相，海水不可斗量　People cannot be judged by their appearance; oceans cannot be measured with a bucket

- 《初刻拍案惊奇》• 凌濛初 *Slapping the Table in Amazement*, by Ling Mengchu (1580–1644 CE)
  留得青山在，不怕没柴烧　Keep the mountain green so you'll have firewood to burn

4. Miscellaneous works:

- 《韩诗外传》• 韩婴 *Han's Exegeses on the Classic of Poetry*, by Han Ying (ca. 200–130 BCE)
  伯乐相马　Bo Le recognizes a superb horse

- 《为东魏檄梁文》• 杜弼 "Proclamation Issued to Liang on Behalf of Eastern Wei," by Du Bi, 547 CE
  城门失火，殃及池鱼　When the city gate burns, fish in the moat will suffer disaster

- 《马说》• 韩愈 "Philosophy about Horses," by Han Yu (768–824 CE)
  伯乐相马　Bo Le recognizes a superb horse

- 《历代名画记》• 张彦远 *Record of Famous Paintings from the Past*, by Zhang Yan-yuan (815–907 CE)
  画龙点睛　Painting the eyes on a dragon

- 《文与可画篔筜谷偃竹记》• 苏轼 "Memoir of Wen Yuke Painting Bamboos at the Tall Bamboo Valley," by Su Shi, 1079 CE
  胸有成竹　Holding a fully-formed bamboo in his heart

An Alphabetical List
of the Chinese Sayings

This list is ordered alphabetically by the Chinese sayings written in *pinyin*.

Marking a Boat to Locate a Lost Sword

In many cultures of the world in olden times, it was the fashion for men to carry a sword, whether or not it was a practical necessity. In ancient China, there was a tradition where men carried a sword as a sign of social status. This story is about a man who took great pride in his sword.

Before China became a unified empire in 221 BCE, it was divided into many states. This man lived in Chu—a vast sprawling state straddling the Yangtze River and its myriad tributaries. At the height of its glory, the state of Chu encompassed present-day Shanghai and Chongqing.

One day this man decided to go visit a friend who lived in a village on the other side of the river. On the morning of his visit, he walked out of the house without his precious sword. His wife, who was much more alert than he was, yelled out to him "Hey! You forgot your sword!" With a smile of relief, the man went back to get it. As he left the house again, his wife said to him, "Be careful crossing the river and don't forget your sword when you come home!" The man then proceeded down to the river's edge. He soon reached the spot where the ferries were docked and saw that he had several to choose from.

The boatmen called out to travelers:
"Best ferry service to the other side!" said the first.
"Fastest ferry boat right here!"said another.
"This ferry is the newest model; it will give you the smoothest ride!" chimed a third.

One old boatman called out to him, "Here sir, my boat may not be the fastest or the smoothest, but it is very steady and I'll give you the best price." It took the man only a moment to realize that this old boatman needed the business the most, so he decided to take his ferry.

The ride was pleasant enough until suddenly, about halfway across the river, the water became choppy. The ferry rocked from side to side. All of a sudden, the man lost his grip on his sword and it fell into the river with a splash.

"Stop!" he yelled, "My sword fell overboard!"

刻舟求剑

古时候，在很多国家男人都喜欢身上带着剑，不管这把剑有没有用。中国也一样，男人出门带着剑是一种社会地位的<u>象征</u>。我们现在就讲一个男人和剑的故事。

<u>公元前</u>221年以前，中国还不是一个统一的国家，还是很多不同的小国家。故事里的这个男人住在楚国。那时候楚国很大，也很<u>强盛</u>，长江<u>中下游</u>从今天的重庆到上海这么一大片土地，在那个时候都是楚国的。

有一天，男人要到河对面去看一个朋友。早上出门的时候，他<u>竟然</u>忘了带剑。他太太比他细心多了，冲着他大叫了一声："喂！你忘了带剑了！"这时候男人才想起来，赶紧回去取了剑。再出门的时候，太太又说："过河的时候你要小心一点儿，记得把剑带回来！"男人出门走到了河边，那里停着几条船。

船夫们都大声地<u>吆喝</u>：
"到河对岸最好的服务在这里哈！"
"来呀，最快的船在这里！"
"我的船最新，坐起来最舒服！"

一个老船夫冲着男人说："先生，我的船可能不是最快的，也不是最舒服的，但是很<u>稳</u>，也最便宜，坐我的船吧！"男人看得出来老人最需要赚钱，于是就决定坐老人的船。

男人上了船。快到河中间的时候，水突然变得很急，船也左右摇晃了起来。突然，男人一<u>松手</u>，剑掉进了河里。

男人大叫了一声："快停下来！我的剑掉下去了！"

The boatman stopped the boat for a moment while the man peered down into the murky water for his sword. Sadly, there was no sign of it. He was quite distraught but then he had an idea. He decided to carve a notch on the side of the boat where his sword had gone overboard. He did this with a little knife that he always kept in his pocket and he did it surreptitiously as he thought to himself, "When we reach more shallow water, I'll jump into the water where I made this mark. That way, I should be able to find my sword." All this time, the boatman kept his eye on the water, trying to keep his boat steady, so he did not notice what his passenger was doing.

As the ferry neared the other side of the river, the man rolled up his pant legs and jumped into the water.

"What on earth are you doing?!" cried the boatman, thinking that the man was trying to jump off the ferry without paying.

When the man explained his plan for finding his sword, the boatman doubled over with laughter but then quickly composed himself and said with a straight face, "Sir, with all due respect for a man of your stature, I regret to inform you that the boat has long since left the spot where your sword fell into the water! You'll never find it this way!"

This story later gave birth to the proverb "Carving a boat to find a sword." It is used to epitomize people who are stuck in their ways, oblivious to changing times. In so many aspects of contemporary life, it is important to keep up with the times. Technological developments and globalization have certainly shown that this proverb is as true today as it ever was!

船夫把船停了下来，男人看着<u>浑浊</u>的河水，想找到那把剑，可是看来看去，根本找不到。男人很着急，于是想到了一个主意。他要在船边上，剑掉下去的那个地方刻一个记号。他拿出身上带着的一把小刀，认认真真地刻了一个记号，然后<u>自言自语</u>地说："等船靠岸了，我就从这个记号这里下去找，一定能找到。"这时候，老船夫一心一意地划着船，也没注意男人在做什么。

　　船快靠岸的时候，男人卷起裤脚，跳进了河里。

　　船夫以为男人不想付钱就要离开，就大叫了一声："你干什么？"

　　男人告诉船夫他跳下河是为了去找剑，船夫几乎笑出声来，但他<u>假装</u>没什么事儿，<u>礼貌</u>地跟男人说："<u>尊贵</u>的大人，我们早就离开剑掉下去的地方了，您这样是根本找不到剑的！"

　　这就是"刻舟求剑"的故事。中国人用这个故事来<u>比喻</u>有的人非常<u>刻板守旧</u>，<u>一成不变</u>。在我们今天的生活中，<u>与时俱进</u>是很重要的。科技的发展与全球化都证明，只会"刻舟求剑"的人一定会被社会<u>淘汰</u>的。

The Chinese Proverb

刻	舟	求	剑
kè	zhōu	qiú	jiàn
to carve	a boat	to seek	a sword

Literal meaning: Carving the side of a boat to find a lost sword

Connotation: It is foolish to mark a moving object to locate the position of something. This is a metaphor for adhering rigidly to traditional or conventional thinking when the situation is changing.

The original source: The Annals of Lǚ, Observations of Current Times (third century BCE)《吕氏春秋 • 察今》

Vocabulary

1.	象征	**xiàngzhēng**	to symbolize; symbol, emblem
2.	公元前	**gōngyuánqián**	BCE (Before the Common Era)
3.	强盛	**qiángshèng**	strong and flourishing (re. a nation)
4.	中下游	**zhōngxià-yóu**	middle and lower reaches (of a river)
5.	竟然	**jìngrán**	surprisingly, actually
6.	吆喝	**yāohe**	to call out loudly (i.e., hawkers)
7.	稳	**wěn**	steady
8.	摇晃	**yáohuang**	to sway or rock
9.	松手	**sōngshǒu**	to loosen one's grip, let go
10.	浑浊	**húnzhuó**	muddy, turbid

The Proverb in Modern Usage

Modern Wives and Traditional Husbands

The current generation of well-educated women tends to juggle their traditional roles while aspiring to professional achievement. In today's society, if a man hopes that his wife will be content to be a devoted stay-at-home wife and mother, isn't he just as foolish as the man of Chu who carved a boat to find his lost sword?

Discussion questions (discuss in English or Chinese):

1. As we all know, ancient China was very much a stratified society. Can you describe how that is reflected in the relationship between the man and his wife, and the way the boatman related to the man?

2. As the author of this story sees it, how does social rank correlate with intelligence and ability? How does he satirize the upper class?

3. Describe a situation that you have personally witnessed in which someone behaved in a "carving the boat to find the sword" way.

11.	自言自语	**zìyán zìyǔ**	talking to oneself
12.	假装	**jiǎzhuāng**	to pretend
13.	礼貌	**lǐmào**	polite
14.	尊贵	**zūnguì**	honorable
15.	比喻	**bǐyù**	a metaphor, analogy; to draw a metaphor
16.	刻板守旧	**kèbǎn shǒujiù**	inflexible and conservative
17.	一成不变	**yìchéng búbiàn**	unalterable once established
18.	与时俱进	**yǔshí jù-jìn**	keep advancing with the times
19.	淘汰	**táotài**	to be eliminated through competition, to be weeded out

---

成语今用实例

现代妻子与传统丈夫

当代受过良好教育的女性一般都会追求事业上的成就。在今天的社会上，如果一个男人期望自己的妻子<u>心甘情愿</u>呆在家里当<u>贤妻良母</u>，那他不就是跟那个刻舟求剑的楚人一样<u>愚蠢</u>吗？

....

Vocabulary

20.	心甘情愿	**xīngān qíngyuàn**	perfectly willing
21.	贤妻良母	**xiánqī liángmǔ**	good wife and mother
22.	愚蠢	**yúchǔn**	foolish, stupid

Learning the Handan Walk

In Chinese history, the Warring States period (475–221 BCE) was a time when many feudal lords vied for supremacy. By 260 BCE, the number of feudal states had dwindled from over a hundred to just seven. Among them were Yan and Zhao, the two states mentioned in the present story. The state of Yan, located around present-day Beijing, was the oldest of the seven. The rival state of Zhao, situated to the south of Yan, was an up-and-coming state at the time and its capital Handan remains one of the biggest cities in Hebei province today. Handan is about 270 miles from Beijing; these days, the high-speed train takes only two hours to travel between these two cities.

The story "Learning the Handan Walk" is about a young man from the state of Yan who went to Handan to learn to walk like the Handanese. Why would he do such a bizarre thing? Well, by the end of the Warring States period, the state of Zhao was more advanced than its neighbors. It was politically unified, it had a strong military, and its culture was flourishing. Therefore, it became a model for its neighbors. Rumor had it that the Handanese were beautiful, danced well, and even their walk was very graceful!

Hearing all this, a young man of Yan grew envious of the Handanese and decided to go there to learn their walk. There was no high speed train in those days, so it took this young man many days of walking to reach Handan. Once there, he was out on the street day after day, studying the way the Handanese walked. He walked just a few steps behind his unsuspecting models, slavishly imitating each step. But no matter how hard he practiced, he still could not walk like a Handanese. The young man became really frustrated and depressed. But what's worse, he even forgot how he himself used to walk! Now he was really in trouble! How was he going to return to his home in the state of Yan? Well, in the end, he had to simply crawl home on all fours.

邯郸学步

中国历史上的战国时期（公元前475–221年）群雄争霸。到了公元前260年，只剩下七个诸侯国了，而这个故事说的燕国和赵国就是其中的两个诸侯国。燕国地处今天的北京一带，是七个诸侯国中最早建立政权的。赵国位于燕国南边，在当时是日渐繁荣的新兴诸侯国，而国都邯郸至今还是河北省的大城市之一。邯郸离北京大约270英里，现在坐高铁只要两个小时就到了。

　　"邯郸学步"说的是一个燕国少年到邯郸去学走路的故事。那么，这个少年为什么要从燕国到邯郸去学走路呢？战国后期，赵国跟邻国相比，政治和谐，军事强大，文化繁荣，因此成了邻国学习的榜样。据说，那个时候的邯郸人长得很漂亮，跳舞跳得很好，走路也走得很优雅。

　　燕国少年听说了以后，很羡慕，就决定到邯郸去学走路。那时候从燕国到邯郸可没有高铁，燕国少年走呀走呀，终于到了邯郸。从那以后，他整天在街上看邯郸人走路，见一个学一个，跟在别人后面亦步亦趋。可是不管他怎么努力，还是不能跟邯郸人走得一模一样。燕国少年很难过，更让他伤心的是，他不但没有学会邯郸人走路，还忘了自己原来是怎么走的。这下子可糟糕了，他怎么回燕国老家呢？最后，他只能爬着回去了。

This story is found in a chapter called "The Floods of Autumn" in the book of *Zhuangzi*. Zhuangzi was a leading philosopher and writer of the Warring States period, and one of the most notable figures of the Daoist school of philosophy. His writings are full of imagination, humor and wit. "Learning the Handan Walk" is an example of how Zhuangzi used simple stories to convey profound philosophical ideas. His writings have been hailed as "philosophical literature, and literary philosophy." Historically, there was probably never a young man of Yan who went to Handan to learn to walk, but Zhuangzi used this amusing story to caution people against blindly imitating others lest they end up failing to learn the others' skills, while losing their own in the process.

"邯郸学步"的故事出自《庄子·秋水》。庄子是战国时期的哲学家和文学家，也是中国道家学派最重要的代表人物之一。庄子的想象力很丰富，语言幽默风趣。庄子写的很多像"邯郸学步"一样的故事看起来很简单，但都很巧妙地表达了中国文化中很深的哲理。因此，庄子的文章堪称"文学的哲学，哲学的文学。"历史上可能并没有燕国少年真的到邯郸去学走路，但是庄子用了这个生动的故事来说明一个人在学习的时候，千万不能盲目地模仿别人，不然有可能学不会别人的技能，还把自己原来的本事也丢掉了。

The Chinese Proverb

邯 郸　　　　　学　　步
Hándān　　　　**xué**　　**bù**
Handan (place name)　to learn　steps

Literal meaning: Learning the Handan walk.

Connotation: It is foolhardy to try and mimic a way of doing things that is foreign to one's own circumstances.

The original source: "Floods of Autumn," a chapter in *Zhuangzi* (4th–3rd century BCE) 《庄子•秋水》

Vocabulary

1.	群雄争霸	**qúnxióng zhēngbà**	rival feudal lords vied for supremacy
2.	诸侯国	**zhūhóu-guó**	feudal state
3.	地处	**dìchǔ**	to be situated at
4.	位于	**wèiyú**	to be located at
5.	日渐繁荣	**rìjiàn fánróng**	becoming increasingly prosperous
6.	新兴	**xīnxīng**	newly arisen
7.	高铁	**gāotiě**	high-speed train
8.	少年	**shàonián**	youth
9.	邻国	**línguó**	neighboring country
10.	和谐	**héxié**	harmonious
11.	榜样	**bǎngyàng**	model, example
12.	优雅	**yōuyǎ**	elegant
13.	羡慕	**xiànmù**	to admire, to envy
14.	亦步亦趋	**yì-bù-yì-qū**	to imitate slavishly
15.	一模一样	**yì-mó-yí-yàng**	to be exactly alike
16.	道家	**Dàojiā**	Daoist school of thought
17.	学派	**xuépài**	school of thought

18.	幽默风趣	**yōumò fēngqù**	humorous and witty
19.	巧妙	**qiǎomiào**	ingenious, clever
20.	哲理	**zhélǐ**	philosophical theory
21.	堪称	**kānchēng**	worthy to be called
22.	生动	**shēngdòng**	lively, vivid
23.	盲目	**mángmù**	blindly
24.	模仿	**mófǎng**	to imitate
25.	技能	**jìnéng**	techniques, skills
26.	本事	**běnshi**	ability

China Opens to the World

At the end of 1978, China began implementing a policy of internal reform and re-opened its doors to the outside world. At this time China was economically backward, especially when compared with the developed nations of the West. Some Chinese advocated a wholesale adoption of Western ways. But others, who felt Western ways were not necessarily suited to China's conditions, disagreed. Their argument was that if China indiscriminately modeled herself after the West, the result would be like trying to learn the Handan walk. History has shown that China made the correct choice by following her own path of development. Today, China has been transformed from an over-populated, poor and backward nation into the world's second largest economic power.

Discussion questions (discuss in English or Chinese):

1. One could argue that there is a flip side to the "Learning the Handan Walk" story. In our modern, multi-cultural society, learning from other cultures is considered a good thing. After all, good ideas should flourish everywhere. Can you think of two scenarios, one that fits the message of the "Learning the Handan Walk" story and one that illustrates the opposite side of that message?

2. Are there any allegories in Western culture similar to the "Learning the Handan Walk" story? What sort of moral message do they convey?

3. There is another common saying in Chinese: "Adopt others' strong points to supplement one's own shortcomings." In our quest for self-improvement, how can we profit from this saying, while avoiding the pitfalls of "Learning the Handan Walk"?

中国在对外开放初期的<u>抉择</u>

1978年末，中国打开了国门，实行对内改革，对外开放的政策。那时候的中国跟西方发达国家相比，经济上很<u>落后</u>。当时，一些人认为中国应该<u>全盘西化</u>，把西方的做法都搬到中国来；可是另一些人不同意，觉得西方的做法不一定适合中国的国情，如果完全<u>照搬</u>西方的<u>模式</u>，就可能会出现邯郸学步的结果。事实证明，中国<u>坚持</u>走自己的发展道路是<u>正确</u>的选择。如今，中国已经从一个人口<u>众多</u>，<u>贫穷</u>落后的大国发展成为了世界第二大<u>经济体</u>。

Vocabulary

27.	抉择	**juézé**	choice, decision
28.	落后	**luòhòu**	backward; to fall behind
29.	全盘西化	**quánpán xīhuà**	to Westernize totally
30.	照搬	**zhàobān**	indiscriminately imitate
31.	模式	**móshì**	model, pattern
32.	坚持	**jiānchí**	to persist, to insist
33.	正确	**zhèngquè**	correct
34.	众多	**zhòngduō**	numerous, massive
35.	贫穷	**pínqióng**	poor
36.	经济体	**jīngjìtǐ**	economic entity

Like a Frog at the Bottom of a Well

The story "Like a Frog at the Bottom of a Well" has a very interesting historical background. During the Warring States period, two famous men—Gongsun Long and Wei Mou—were originally good friends. Gongsun Long was a philosopher known for his debating skills while Wei Mou, a devotee of the philosopher Zhuangzi, was a prince from the minor state of Zhongshan.

One day Gongsun Long sought Wei Mou's advice about a quandary that had been bothering him. Instead of asking straightforwardly, however, Gongsun Long took this approach to his question: "I've been studying the books of the ancient sages since I was young and have become quite a learned man. I can argue and turn something that's wrong into something that's right. When I engage others in debate, I often leave them speechless. I can even make intelligent people feel befuddled. So why is it that I feel confused when I hear Zhuangzi's discourse? How can it be that my knowledge is no match for his?"

Hearing his friend speak with such bravado, Wei Mou heaved a deep sigh then looked up at heaven and laughed out loud as he replied, "Have you heard the story about the frog in the well?"

One day a frog who lived in an abandoned well said to the giant turtle of the Eastern Sea, "Look at me, I'm the happiest creature in this world! I can come up whenever I want and hop around the rim of the well. When I get tired, I can rest on a ledge on the inside wall. When I jump into the water, it buoys me up. When I walk through a mud puddle, it covers my feet. When I look at the other creatures around me—the little bugs, baby crabs and tadpoles—none of them is as happy as me! What's more, I am the lord of this well with all its delights! You really should come down and see it for yourself!"

井底之蛙

"井底之蛙"这个故事的历史背景很有意思。话说战国时期有两位名人，一位叫公孙龙，另一位叫魏牟。这两个人原来是好朋友。据说，公孙龙能言善辩，而魏牟曾经是中山国的王子，后来很崇拜庄子。有一天，公孙龙去找魏牟请教一个问题。公孙龙说："我从小就学习古代圣贤的书，觉得自己算是很有学问的人了。我能把不对的说成对的，跟别人辩论的时候，别人常常无话可说。我还能让聪明的人觉得困惑。但是，为什么我听了庄子的言谈就觉得很茫然呢？难道我的学问不如庄子吗？"魏牟听了公孙龙这番自夸的话，先叹了一口气，然后仰头笑着说："你没听说过'井底之蛙'的故事吗？"

一口废井里的青蛙对来自东海的大鳖说："你看我好快乐啊！我总是开心地在井口的栏杆上跳来跳去，累了就在井壁的砖缝里休息一下。我跳到水里可以浮在水面上，走在泥里泥水就盖住我的脚背。我回头看看水里的那些小虫，小蟹和蝌蚪，谁能有我这么快乐呢？再说，这整口井都属于我自己，你真应该下来自己体验一下！"

Hearing all this made the great turtle curious, so he decided to go down into the well to take a look. But even before he could put in his left foot, his right knee got stuck on the rim of the well. So the great turtle slowly backed out and began telling the frog about the Eastern Sea.

"You let me look at your well," said the great turtle, "so now I'll tell you about the Eastern Sea. This sea is so vast that even a distance of a thousand *li* cannot begin to describe its breadth and the height of a thousand poles is not enough to measure its depth! In ancient times, the earth was once ravaged by floods for nine years out of ten and yet the sea did not rise one bit. At another time, there were droughts seven years out of eight and the sea did not change one bit. Thus the Eastern Sea is not affected by the changing times and it does not expand or shrink according to the amount of rainfall. This is the greatest delight of the Eastern Sea!" Hearing what the great turtle just said, the frog was stunned and was left utterly speechless.

Having finished his story, Wei Mou continued, "You sir are quite a learned man but you are still not capable of comprehending the profundity of Zhuangzi's philosophy. You are like a gnat trying to carry a great mountain on its back. It's totally impossible! You might as well be gone. Otherwise you might turn into that young man who tried to learn the Handan walk.* Not only did he fail to walk like the Handanese, he even forgot his own original walk and ended up crawling home on his hands and knees!"

---

* The story of the young man who tried to walk like a Handanese is in Chapter 2. In fact, both stories come from the same source.

大鳖听了青蛙的话，有点儿好奇，就想自己到井里看看。不过呢，大鳖的左脚还没进去，右膝就在井外边绊住了。于是，大鳖只好慢慢退了出来，跟青蛙讲起了东海的情形。

　　大鳖说：“你让我看了井，那我给你讲讲东海吧。东海可大了，一千里的距离还没有它那么广大，把一千个长杆子叠加在一起也没有它那么深！在远古的时候，十年里有九年发生了涝灾，海水都没有增加一分，在另一个远古时期，八年里有七年遇上了大旱，海水也没有减少一分。所以呀，东海不会因为大环境的变化而变化，也不会因为雨量的多少而增减，这就是东海最大的快乐！”听完大鳖的话，青蛙目瞪口呆，一句话也说不出来了。

魏年接着跟公孙龙说：“虽然你公孙龙的学问不错了，但是凭你现在的能力，要了解庄子玄妙深奥的哲理，就好像让一只蚊虫去背一座大山，那是肯定不可能的。你还是赶紧走吧，不然你就会像那个燕国少年去邯郸学步一样，学不会邯郸人走路，还把自己的那点本事都给忘了，到头来只能爬着回去了！”

The Chinese Proverb

井	底	之	蛙
jǐng	**dǐ**	**zhī**	**wā**
well	bottom	(preposition)	frog

Literal meaning: The frog at the bottom of a well

Connotation: A person with a very limited outlook who takes pride in his own ignorant complacency.

The original source: "Floods of Autumn," a chapter in *Zhuangzi* (4th-3rd century BCE) 《庄子·秋水》

Vocabulary

1. 能言善辩　**néngyán shànbiàn**　skillful at speaking and debating
2. 崇拜　**chóngbài**　to worship, to revere
3. 圣贤　**shèngxián**　sage
4. 学问　**xuéwen**　knowledge, learning
5. 无话可说　**wú huà kě shuō**　to have nothing to say, to be speechless
6. 困惑　**kùnhuò**　befuddled, perplexed
7. 茫然　**mángrán**　at a loss, in the dark
8. 自夸　**zìkuā**　to boast
9. 叹气　**tànqì**　to sigh
10. 仰头　**yǎngtóu**　to raise one's head, to look upward
11. 废井　**fèijǐng**　abandoned well
12. 鳖　**biē**　turtle
13. 壁　**bì**　wall
14. 砖缝　**zhuānfèng**　crevice between the bricks
15. 浮　**fú**　to float, to buoy
16. 属于　**shǔyú**　to belong to
17. 体验　**tǐyàn**　to experience firsthand
18. 好奇　**hàoqí**　to be curious
19. 膝　**xī**　knee

20.	绊住	**bànzhù**	to be entangled or stuck
21.	叠加	**diéjiā**	to pile up
22.	涝灾	**làozāi**	flood
23.	大旱	**dàhàn**	great drought
24.	目瞪口呆	**mùdèng kǒudāi**	stupefied
25.	凭	**píng**	on the basis of
26.	玄妙深奥	**xuánmiào shēn'ào**	abstruse and profound
27.	哲理	**zhélǐ**	philosophic theories
28.	背	**bēi**	to carry on the back
29.	本事	**běnshi**	skill, ability
30.	到头来	**dào tóu lái**	in the end

A Country Boy Becomes a Scholar

A certain American sinologist was born and raised in a remote farming community. He had a happy childhood, but it was not until he went to college that he had much contact with the outside world. At that point however, his horizons suddenly widened and he realized he had been a frog in a well. In graduate school, he dedicated himself to studying Chinese language and history. Eventually he became an accomplished scholar. After his retirement he revisited his hometown and discovered to his great surprise that his grandfather had produced rich historical records about his hometown. Thereupon he exclaimed with a sigh, "The great turtle of the Eastern Sea doesn't necessarily understand the life of the frog in a well either. Perhaps we humans, each in our own way, are all like frogs in a well!"

....

Discussion (in English or Chinese):

1. We have all known someone who behaves like a frog in a well. Can you describe one or two from your own experience?

2. Has this story inspired you to do something differently to prevent yourself from being called a frog in a well?

3. There's another Chinese saying: 读万卷书，行千里路 **dú wànjuàn shū, xíng qiānlǐ lù** "read 10,000 books, travel 1000 leagues." Without looking it up, what do you think it means? In your opinion, which of the two phrases in this saying is more important?

从美国农村走出来的汉学家

一位美国汉学家出生在一个偏僻的农村里，并在那里度过了愉快的童年。直到上了大学，他才真正接触到外面的世界，开阔了眼界。他觉得自己从前就像一只井底之蛙。上了研究所以后，他潜心学习中文，研究中国历史，成为了有成就的汉学家。退休之后，他又回到农场小镇，惊讶地发现了自己祖先丰富的历史记载。汉学家因此感叹，东海大鳖也不一定了解井底之蛙的全部生活，而人类有时候都是自己主观世界的井底之蛙。

Vocabulary

31.	农村	**nóngcūn**	farming village
32.	汉学家	**Hànxué-jiā**	sinologist
33.	偏僻	**piānpì**	remote, out of the way
34.	接触	**jiēchù**	to come into contact with
35.	开阔眼界	**kāikuò yǎnjiè**	to open up one's field of vision
36.	潜心	**qiánxīn**	to concentrate on (lit. "to immerse one's heart in")
37.	惊讶	**jīngyà**	surprised, startled
38.	感叹	**gǎntàn**	to sigh with emotion
39.	主观	**zhǔguān**	subjective

The Bamboo Painter with Real Bamboo in His Heart

The most admirable human virtues in Chinese culture are symbolized by four plants—plum, orchid, chrysanthemum and bamboo. Bamboo symbolizes the virtues of resilience, honor, simplicity and modesty. So naturally it is a favorite subject in Chinese art—and those who can paint it well are presumed to possess its virtues as well. This is the true story of Wen Yuke, an eccentric artist who "had real bamboo in his heart," as told by his cousin Su Shi (1037–1101), a renowned poet of the Song dynasty.

Like virtually all famous poets and artists in Chinese history, the artist Wen Yuke (1018–1079) made a living as a government official. He held a rather undistinguished post in a poor backwater area in present-day Shaanxi province, but that was just fine with him because bamboo—his passion—grew abundantly in that area. He would often go to a place called Tall Bamboo Valley with his wife to gaze at the bamboo, paint them and enjoy dishes prepared with bamboo shoots. This in itself was not all that unusual. What was eccentric about Wen Yuke was that he wanted to experience the life of the bamboo in all seasons and weather conditions. Under the scorching sun or in the freezing snow, he would be out amongst the bamboo meticulously observing them. His cousin Su Shi visited him at his post and knew that he was a "bamboo fanatic." Su Shi even teased him about it in their correspondence.

But life is unpredictable. Just as Wen Yuke's idyllic life seemed set, he was promoted to a post near the capital. Su Shi was happy at the news and looked forward to spending more time with Yuke, to enjoy drinking, writing poetry and painting together. Unlike other men who focus on advancement, however, Wen Yuke's heart sank, and he fell ill on the way to his new post and passed away.

胸有成竹

在中国文化里，梅、兰、菊、竹分别代表最受人敬重的四种美德，而竹代表的是坚韧、正直、简朴和谦逊。因此，竹子很自然地成为了中国绘画里最常见的一个主题，而人们一般认为能画好竹子的人也有这些美德。"胸有成竹"说的是历史上有点古怪的一位画家的真实故事，而讲故事的人是画家的表弟，宋朝家喻户晓的大文豪苏轼(1037–1101)。

这个成语故事里的画家名叫文与可(1018–1079)。像中国历史上有名的诗人与画家一样，文与可也是靠在朝廷里做官来维持生计。当时，文与可在今天陕西省一个比较偏僻的地方做官，不过他挺开心的，因为那里到处生长着竹子，而文与可对竹子很痴迷。文与可常常和妻子到一个叫做"筼筜谷"的地方去赏竹，画竹，吃用竹笋做的菜。在别人眼里，这都没什么不正常的，而有些古怪的是文与可一年四季的生活都离不开竹子。不管是烈日炎炎还是冰天雪地，文与可都要到竹林里去，仔仔细细地观察竹子在不同的自然环境里的姿态。表弟苏轼曾经到文与可任职的地方拜访过表兄，知道他是个"竹痴"，甚至在他们的通信中拿这件事儿开玩笑。

世事难料。就在文与可安心过着田园生活的时候，却被调往京城附近，升任新的官职。苏轼非常兴奋，期待与表兄一起饮酒赋诗作画，共度更多美好的时光。不过，文与可跟看重官职的人不一样，告别田园生活让他十分难过，结果他在赴任的路上病倒了，不久就去世了。

Grief-stricken, his cousin Su Shi wrote a eulogy to commemorate Wen Yuke and his love of bamboo. In this essay he said "Yuke's approach to painting bamboo can be likened to the way bamboo grows in nature. A one-inch sprout harbors all the elements of a tall, fully-grown bamboo plant. As Yuke prepared to paint bamboo, he first formed the image of an entire real-life bamboo in his mind before he set brush to paper. He focused his gaze on this fully-formed bamboo within his mind's eye, then simply let his brush express that real-life bamboo as it moved onto the paper." His essay goes on to explain that just knowing this principle doesn't make someone a great bamboo painter, for it takes many years of practice for it to become second nature.

As a result of Su Shi's essay, "Holding a fully-formed bamboo in his heart" has come to be a metaphor for "being fully confident about doing something because one already knows it by heart." This also implies that the person or artist has trained himself so thoroughly that the task has become intuitive.

苏轼听到这个消息，万分悲痛，就写了一篇悼文来怀念文与可，以及表兄对竹子深深的爱。在这篇悼文里，苏轼写道："与可画竹就像竹子长在竹林里一样。只是一寸高的初生小芽，就已经看到竹节和竹叶了。与可准备画竹之前，心里已经有了竹子完整的形象。真正下笔的时候，他只要全神贯注地照着心里想的竹子的样子，让画笔在纸上飞舞，一气呵成。"苏轼在悼文里还提到，只知道这个画竹的道理是不能成为大师的，只有不断地练习，技法才能变成一种本能。

从此以后，"胸有成竹"就成了一个比喻，用来指一个人对所要做的事情非常有信心，也就是说这个人凭着本能就能轻而易举地做好那件事情。

The Chinese Proverb

胸	有	成	竹
xiōng	**yǒu**	**chéng**	**zhú**
chest, heart	to have	fully-formed, completed	bamboo

Literal meaning: To have fully-formed bamboo in your heart.

Connotation: (The painter of bamboo) has "a fully-formed image of bamboo" in his mind, implying that painting the bamboo will be intuitive. This is a metaphor for knowing something so well or having practiced a skill so thoroughly that one has complete confidence to do it well because it is second nature.

The original source: "Memoir of Wen Yuke Painting Bamboos at the Tall Bamboo Valley," an essay written by Su Shi in 1079, during the Northern Song dynasty.《文与可画筼筜谷偃竹记》，1079年北宋苏轼著。

Vocabulary

1. 梅　　　**méi**　　　plum
2. 兰　　　**lán**　　　orchid
3. 菊　　　**jú**　　　chrysanthemum
4. 竹　　　**zhú**　　　bamboo
5. 敬重　　**jìngzhòng**　　to respect
6. 美德　　**měidé**　　virtue
7. 坚韧　　**jiānrèn**　　strong and durable, resilient
8. 简朴　　**jiǎnpǔ**　　simple and unadorned
9. 谦逊　　**qiānxùn**　　humble, modest
10. 绘画　　**huìhuà**　　to paint paintings
11. 古怪　　**gǔguài**　　eccentric, odd
12. 表弟　　**biǎodì**　　younger male cousin
13. 家喻户晓　**jiā yù hù xiǎo**　to be a household name
14. 文豪　　**wénháo**　　great literary figure
15. 朝廷　　**cháotíng**　　imperial court, government
16. 维持　　**wéichí**　　to maintain
17. 生计　　**shēngjì**　　livelihood
18. 偏僻　　**piānpì**　　remote, out of the way
19. 痴迷　　**chīmí**　　obsessed, infatuated
20. 筼筜谷　**Yúndāng Gǔ**　Tall Bamboo Valley
21. 赏　　　**shǎng**　　to appreciate, to admire, to enjoy
22. 竹笋　　**zhúsǔn**　　bamboo shoots
23. 烈日炎炎　**lièrì yányán**　scorching sun
24. 冰天雪地　**bīngtiān xuědì**　ice and snow; freezing cold weather
25. 观察　　**guānchá**　　to observe
26. 姿态　　**zītài**　　posture, pose, appearance
27. 任职　　**rènzhí**　　to hold a position

28.	世事难料	**shìshì nánliào**	affairs of the world are hard to predict
29.	田园	**tiányuán**	"field and garden," countryside; pastoral
30.	调往	**diàowǎng**	to be transferred to
31.	升任	**shēngrèn**	to be promoted (professionally)
32.	兴奋	**xīngfèn**	delighted
33.	期待	**qīdài**	to look forward to
34.	赋诗	**fùshī**	to compose poetry
35.	共度···时光	**gòngdù...shíguāng**	to pass time together
36.	告别	**gàobié**	to bid farewell to
37.	赴任	**fùrèn**	to go forth to take up a position
38.	去世	**qùshì**	to pass away, to die
39.	悲痛	**bēitòng**	sorrowful; grief
40.	悼文	**dàowén**	a written or spoken memorial for a deceased person
41.	怀念	**huáiniàn**	to cherish the memory of
42.	芽	**yá**	sprout
43.	节	**jié**	section, joint (in a bamboo stalk)
44.	形象	**xíngxiàng**	image
45.	全神贯注	**quánshén guànzhù**	totally focused, with total concentration
46.	飞舞	**fēiwǔ**	"fly and dance"
47.	一气呵成	**yí-qì-hē-chéng**	to complete in one breath
48.	技法	**jìfǎ**	technique
49.	本能	**běnnéng**	intuitive, second nature
50.	比喻	**bǐyù**	metaphor
51.	凭着	**píngzhe**	on the strength of, to rely on
52.	轻而易举	**qīng ér yì jǔ**	easy to do

Why Risk Failure?

The main story in this chapter might make the reader wonder whether a project should be attempted at all if one has no confidence it will succeed. After all, in many cases certain factors necessary to success are not within one's control. For example, even an outstanding writer might not be able to find a publisher for her work. Successful works of art or literature often begin with just passion and perseverance. Every artist or writer has a great deal of doubt, but believes that risking failure and trying one's best is worthwhile in itself. It is also said that "failure is the mother of success." Of course, embarking on a task without confidence should be done only when failure does not bring dire consequences. A student should definitely make every effort to prepare as thoroughly as possible for an exam, because the confidence from "holding a real bamboo in her heart" will in itself allow her to perform to the best of her ability.

Discussion questions (discuss in English or Chinese):

1. Given your current Chinese abilities, what things do you feel you can do in a Chinese language environment with confidence? What things do you feel you have no confidence doing in such an environment?

2. How would you advise a young friend in China who is about to face the dreaded college entrance exams: to make the most of the day before the exam to review everything, or to take the day off and go to bed early? Is your advice related to the notion of "holding a fully formed bamboo in the heart"?

3. What kind of people might fail despite "holding a fully formed bamboo in the heart"? What kind of people are the just the opposite? Do you personally know both kinds of people? Share some examples and compare them.

为何冒失败的风险

这个故事或许会让读者思考这样一个问题：在"胸无成竹"的情况下，一个人是不是应该努力尝试做一件事呢？在很多情况下，决定能否成功的因素并不在个人的掌控中。例如，即使是一位优秀的作家也不一定能找到一位出版商来出版他的作品。成功的艺术或文学作品往往始于激情和恒心。艺术家或者作家一开始也会怀疑自己能不能成功，但同时又相信，冒着失败的风险尽最大的努力本身是有价值的。"失败是成功之母"嘛。当然，只有在失败不会造成灭顶之灾的前提下，一个人才应该在没有成功把握的时候去冒险。一个学生考试以前一定得尽最大的努力做好准备，毕竟"胸有成竹"才能在考试时让一个人发挥得最好。

Vocabulary

53.	冒…风险	mào...fēngxiǎn	to take risk, to take chances (syn. 冒险 màoxiǎn)
54.	失败	shībài	failure; to fail
55.	思考	sīkǎo	to think about, to ponder over
56.	尝试	chángshì	to attempt
57.	能否	néngfǒu	can or cannot
58.	因素	yīnsù	factor
59.	掌控	zhǎngkòng	control; to have under control
60.	即使	jíshǐ	even if
61.	优秀	yōuxiù	outstanding, excellent
62.	出版商	chūbǎnshāng	publisher (commercial)
63.	激情	jīqíng	passion
64.	恒心	héngxīn	perseverance (lit. "enduring heart")
65.	怀疑	huáiyí	to doubt, to suspect
66.	价值	jiàzhí	value
67.	灭顶之灾	mièdǐng zhī zāi	big disaster, great calamity
68.	前提	qiántí	premise
69.	毕竟	bìjìng	after all
70.	发挥	fāhuī	to bring into play (ability, potential, etc.)

Painting the Eyes on a Dragon

During the Liang Dynasty (502–557) there was a famous court painter by the name of Zhang Sengyou (ca. 490–540). This was a time when Buddhism, with all its religious and cultural influences was coming into China from India. Zhang Sengyou was commissioned by the emperor to paint large murals at Buddhist temples in the capital (present-day Nanjing). His works were so esteemed that many of them were replicated by later painters and can now be found in major museums around the world. Some three centuries later in the late Tang dynasty, a notable art historian and collector wrote the following story about one of Zhang Sengyou's works:

> Emperor Wu of the Liang dynasty commissioned Zhang Sengyou to paint four golden dragons on a mural at Anle Temple. It took him only three days to complete the assignment. As expected, the painted dragons were extremely vivid and true to life. The mural attracted throngs of viewers, who all marveled at how lifelike the dragons looked. The only thing was, when they walked up close to see it, they discovered that none of the dragons had eyes! One by one, people pleaded with Zhang Sengyou to remedy this tiny imperfection. Zhang Sengyou's reply was always the same: "It wouldn't be hard at all to put eyes on the dragons, but if I did that, the dragons would crash through the wall and fly away." Of course, no one believed him; they all thought this was just a ridiculous excuse. After a while, people started accusing him of lying. It got to the point where Zhang Sengyou couldn't stand the accusations anymore, so he reluctantly agreed to add eyes to the dragons. But secretly, he planned to add eyes on only two of the dragons so that there would at least be two left on the temple's mural. The day he was to

画龙点睛

张僧繇是南北朝时期梁朝(502–557)著名的宫廷画师，活跃在大约490–540年间。张僧繇生活的年代，正是佛教从印度传入中国，在宗教和文化领域都对中国产生极大影响的时期，而张僧繇则奉朝廷之命在当时京城(今天的南京)里的许多佛寺中绘制大型壁画。张僧繇的绘画艺术广受推崇。直到今天，我们在世界各地的博物馆里还能看到后人临摹的他的画作。经历了三个世纪以后，晚唐时期的一位著名艺术史学家兼收藏家写下了这么一个关于张僧繇的故事：

梁武帝命张僧繇在安乐寺的墙壁上画四条金龙。张僧繇只用了三天就画好了。那四条金龙画得栩栩如生，惟妙惟肖，吸引了很多人前来观看。人人都对画师的手法赞不绝口。不过，当人们走近一看，才发现唯一美中不足的是这几条金龙都没画眼睛！于是，大家就恳请张僧繇把金龙的眼睛点上。张僧繇总是说："给金龙点上眼睛并不难，但我一那样做，这几条金龙就会破壁飞走的。"当然，没有人相信张僧繇的说法，都觉得这样的解释实在有点儿荒唐。后来，有的人甚至说张僧繇不诚实。张僧繇受不了了，就很不情愿地答应了给金龙点上眼睛。不过，他心里计划只给两条金龙点上眼睛，这样至少还有两条金龙会留在佛寺的壁画上。到了张僧繇给金龙点眼睛的那一天，许多人都跑来见证这一时刻。张僧繇拿起画笔，轻轻地给两条金

paint the eyes on the dragons, a crowd gathered to witness the event. As Zhang picked up his brush and lightly added dots for the eyes of two dragons, dark clouds mushroomed overhead, followed by gusts of wind, then a flash of lightning and a clap of thunder. Everyone except Zhang Sengyou was horror-struck by the sight of two fantastic dragons crashing through the mural and soaring into the stormy sky. Then just as quickly, the storm blew over and the clouds cleared up. The crowd stood there with their mouths agape, unable to utter a word. When they looked at the mural again, sure enough only the two dragons without eyes remained. No one knew where the other two had vanished to.

The above story was not intended to be a fairy tale nor was it meant to be taken as factual history. In fact, it comes from a serious historical art treatise called *Record of Famous Paintings from the Past*. The author Zhang Yanyuan (815–907) himself was a highly respected painter, calligrapher, connoisseur and art critic. Most likely, he sensed that a straightforward account could not adequately demonstrate his extraordinary esteem for Zhang Sengyou's work, and that only a legend could do it justice.

龙点上了眼睛。刹那间，天空中乌云翻滚，狂风大作，电闪雷鸣。只见那两条点了眼睛的金龙腾空而起，穿破画壁，飞向了雷电交加的天空中。又过了片刻，云开雾散，好像什么都没发生一样。除了张僧繇以外，围观的人都吓得目瞪口呆，站在那里一句话也说不出来了。大家再往墙壁上一看，壁画上只剩下那两条没点眼睛的金龙了，谁也不知道那两条点了眼睛的金龙飞到哪儿去了。

"画龙点睛"并不是一个编撰出来的神话故事，而是出自《历代名画记》这样一部严肃的艺术史专著。作者张彦远(815–907)本人是一位受人敬仰的画家，书法家，鉴赏家和艺术评论家。画龙点睛的故事显然并不是历史上的真实事件，但在张彦远的心目中，只有撰写这样一个传奇故事，才能最完美地诠释他对张僧繇的敬佩之情。

The Chinese Proverb

画	龙	点	睛
huà	**lóng**	**diǎn**	**jīng**
to paint	a dragon	to dot	the eyes

Literal meaning: To paint the eyes on a dragon.

Connotation: When creating a work of art, it is the finishing touches that bring it to life. In creating a literary work, this refers to the critical passages that capture the spirit and essence of the work. In a discussion, it refers to the final statements that clinch the argument.

The original source: Record of Famous Paintings from the Past, by Zhang Yanyuan (815–907, Tang dynasty) 唐•张彦远《历代名画记•张僧繇》

Vocabulary

1.	宫廷	**gōngtíng**	palace, imperial court
2.	活跃	**huóyuè**	to be active
3.	佛教	**fójiào**	Buddhism
4.	宗教	**zōngjiào**	religion
5.	领域	**lǐngyù**	realm, territory, field
6.	奉...之命	**fèng...zhī mìng**	to do something under the order of ...
7.	朝廷	**cháotíng**	royal court
8.	佛寺	**fósì**	Buddhist temple
9.	绘制	**huìzhì**	to draw (a design, a painting, etc.)
10.	壁画	**bìhuà**	mural
11.	绘画	**huìhuà**	to paint pictures
12.	广受	**guǎngshòu**	widely receiving (acclaim, etc.)
13.	推崇	**tuīchóng**	to hold in esteem
14.	临摹	**línmó**	to copy (a model of painting or calligraphy)
15.	兼	**jiān**	to hold another position concurrently
16.	收藏家	**shōucángjiā**	collector (of art, etc.)
17.	栩栩如生	**xǔxǔ rúshēng**	lifelike
18.	惟妙惟肖	**wéimiào wéixiào**	remarkably true to life

19.	吸引	**xīyǐn**	to attract
20.	手法	**shǒufǎ**	technique
21.	赞不绝口	**zàn bù jué kǒu**	to praise profusely
22.	美中不足	**měizhōng bùzú**	a blemish in an otherwise perfect thing
23.	恳请	**kěnqǐng**	to earnestly request
24.	破壁	**pòbì**	to break through the wall
25.	荒唐	**huāngtáng**	absurd, preposterous
26.	诚实	**chéngshí**	honest
27.	情愿	**qíngyuàn**	willing
28.	见证	**jiànzhèng**	to witness
29.	时刻	**shíkè**	moment
30.	刹那间	**chà'nàjiān**	in an instant
31.	乌云翻滚	**wūyún fāngǔn**	dark clouds churning
32.	狂风大作	**kuángfēng dàzuò**	fierce wind breaking out
33.	电闪雷鸣	**diànshǎn léimíng**	flash of lightning and roar of thunder
34.	腾空而起	**téngkōng ér qǐ**	soared up to the sky
35.	穿破	**chuānpò**	to break through
36.	雷电交加	**léidiàn jiāojiā**	thunder and lightning came one after another
37.	片刻	**piànkè**	a short while
38.	云开雾散	**yúnkāi wùsàn**	clouds scattered and fog dissipated
39.	目瞪口呆	**mùdèng kǒudāi**	stupefied, dumbstruck
40.	编撰	**biānzhuàn**	to write, to compile (a book)
41.	神话	**shénhuà**	fairy tale
42.	严肃	**yánsù**	serious
43.	专著	**zhuānzhù**	treatise, book on a special subject
44.	敬仰	**jìngyǎng**	to venerate
45.	鉴赏家	**jiànshǎngjiā**	connoisseur
46.	评论家	**pínglùnjiā**	critic
47.	撰写	**zhuànxiě**	to write
48.	传奇	**chuánqí**	legend
49.	诠释	**quánshì**	to elucidate
50.	敬佩	**jìngpèi**	to esteem, to admire

The Importance of Book Titles

Although the saying "Painting the eyes on the dragon" originally referred to a work of art, it was applied more often to literary works in later times. In the creative process, literary works often take on a life of their own and develop in ways that are surprising even to their creators. Many elements come together to bring a literary work to life, but in some cases it is the title that especially stands out. To readers, the title may seem enigmatic and intriguing at the outset, and it is only at the end that they realize it is indeed "the eyes that the author has painted on the dragon." This point can be illustrated by Shakespeare's plays. Two genres—the histories and tragedies—have names of protagonists as their titles. But the third genre—the comedies—have whimsical titles like *Midsummer Night's Dream, Much Ado about Nothing, Comedy of Errors, Love's Labour's Lost* and *As You Like It*. These titles truly capture the spirit and essence of the plays, and are another mark of Shakespeare's genius.

书名的意义

虽然"画龙点睛"最早出自一件艺术作品，但后来却更多地使用在文学作品中。文学作品在创作的过程中往往形成自己的生命力，以至于其作者在完成创作时都感到十分惊讶。一部文学作品的生命力是由很多因素决定的，而有时候，作品的名字会起到显著的作用。封面上的名字可能会让读者又好奇又纳闷，而只有看完这部作品才发现它的名字确实是作者画龙点睛之笔。莎士比亚的剧作可以用来说明这一点。他的历史剧和悲剧都是用剧中主角命名的；而第三类的剧作，就是喜剧，如《仲夏夜之梦》、《无事生非》、《错误喜剧》、《爱的徒劳》和《皆大欢喜》的剧名都很风趣。可以说这些剧名真实地反映了剧作的精髓，并且充分展现了莎翁的创作天赋。

Vocabulary

51.	出自	chūzì	arise from
52.	作品	zuòpǐn	work (of art, writing, etc.)
53.	过程	guòchéng	process
54.	形成	xíngchéng	to form
55.	生命力	shēngmìnglì	life force, vitality
56.	以至于	yǐ zhìyú	even to the point of ...
57.	惊讶	jīngyà	surprised, amazed
58.	因素	yīnsù	factor, element
59.	起···作用	qǐ...zuòyòng	to have an effect
60.	显著	xiǎnzhù	notable, striking
61.	封面	fēngmiàn	cover (of a book)
62.	纳闷	nàmèn	puzzled, perplexed
63.	···之笔	...zhī bǐ	stroke of the pen
64.	剧作	jùzuò	play, drama
65.	悲剧	bēijù	tragedy
66.	主角	zhǔjué	protagonist
67.	命名	mìngmíng	to bestow a name on (someone or something)
68.	喜剧	xǐjù	comedy (drama)
69.	风趣	fēngqù	witty, humorous
70.	反映	fǎnyìng	to reflect
71.	精髓	jīngsuǐ	quintessence
72.	展现	zhǎnxiàn	to manifest
73.	莎翁	Shā Wēng	Old Master Shakespeare
74.	天赋	tiānfù	talent, genius

Discussion questions (discuss in English or Chinese). Choose 2–3 questions from this list:

1. Imagine yourself at a writers workshop, having a discussion with a small group of colleagues about your struggles trying to finish your work. How would you and your colleagues support each other in the final stage of your writing?

2. Can you think of some other literary works, from any era and any culture, where the title can be considered the "eyes that have been dotted on the dragon"?

3. Have you ever written a masterpiece that you are especially proud of? Can you describe the stroke that "dotted the eyes on the dragon"?

4. The proverb in this chapter elevated the outstanding painter Zhang Sengyou to a legend. Can you think of an artist or writer in the West who has been similarly glorified?

5. Another favorite Chinese saying is 画蛇添足 **huà shé tiān zú** "to draw a snake and add feet to it." Look up this saying and compare it with the saying in this chapter.

The Great Teacher Who Provided Equal Opportunities for His Students

When the average Westerner is asked what he knows about Confucius, he might say that Confucius was the most venerated philosopher in ancient China—perhaps on a par with Plato or Socrates in Western culture. But to the younger generation of Chinese today, Confucius is best known as a great teacher. Confucius' birthday is designated as Teachers' Day to honor Confucius as well as all the teachers in the world.*

This story is about Confucius as a teacher. You may be surprised to learn that he was quite down-to-earth and lovable, not at all stuffy or distant. Quite a few stories about Confucius' interactions with his students have become proverbs. This chapter will recount two favorites.

Confucius was not a teacher in a regular school. He was a master with a group of followers who gathered together, wandering from state to state.† It is said that Confucius had 72 pupils and that they were all very different. He would accept any student who wished to be educated. He gave each student an equal opportunity to study regardless of their social or financial status, intellectual ability or origin. He even accepted "barbarians" (i.e. non-Chinese) and those whose integrity was suspect. One of his pupils—Yan Zhuoju—is said to have been a former robber. To make education affordable for all his students, Confucius charged very little tuition. Not all of his students agreed with this policy. The following story illustrates the controversy.

---

* Teachers' Day is September 10 in China and September 28 in Taiwan. Either way, it comes near the beginning of the school year, which is an appropriate time to steer students toward a respectful attitude toward teachers.
† China was not yet a unified country in Confucius' day. The House of Zhou was officially the ruling dynasty, but in reality it was divided into many big and small feudal states.

有教无类

要是问一个普通的西方人孔子是谁，他很有可能会说孔子是中国文化里最令人敬重的古代哲学家，可以说与西方文化里的柏拉图或者苏格拉底齐名。然而，对今天中国的年轻一代来说，孔子是最伟大的教育家。因此"教师节"就确定在了孔子的诞辰日，以纪念孔子和感恩世界各国的教师们。*这一章我们谈谈孔子是一位什么样的老师。你可能会很惊讶，孔子其实是一位很实在，甚至于可以说很可爱，一点都不古板，也不让人感觉莫测高深的老师。许多孔子与学生之间互动的故事后来都成为了中文里的成语，而这一章就介绍其中两个。

孔子并不是普通学校里的老师。他只是与一群弟子常聚在一起的师傅，从一国周游到另一国。†据说，孔子一共有72位弟子，而这些弟子也是鱼龙混杂。对孔子来说，不管学生的社会地位、经济情况怎么样，也不管他们来自哪里，只要有心向学，他都愿意收为弟子。孔子的学生当中包括夷族，甚至还有人品有问题的学生。有一个学生，名叫颜涿聚，据说就曾经是个强盗。为了让弟子们都上得起学，孔子收的学费很低，但并不是所有的学生都赞同孔子这个做法。下面这个故事说的就是师生间的争议。

---

* 中国大陆与台湾的教师节分别在9月10日与9月28日。这两个日子都定在开学之际，有利于在新学年开始之际就培养学生尊师重道的观念。
† 孔子时代，中国还不是统一的国家。尽管周朝是名义上的统治王朝，但实际上分裂成大大小小的封建制国家。

When Confucius was returning to his home state of Lu with his entourage of students, he discovered to his chagrin that guards had been posted at a checkpoint to collect tolls. He was further embarrassed that he didn't have enough money to pay the toll for all his students, so a student by the name of Zigong generously volunteered to pay for the entire group. Another student Ziwo took this as an opportunity to raise a point with his teacher Confucius saying, "I've told you long ago that you should raise your fees. Your students get their room and board from you, so it's as if you are subsidizing them. Your low tuition is tantamount to letting the well-off students hitch a ride. If you raise your fees, you'll have more money to subsidize the poor students. It's like this checkpoint. I think the country should raise the tolls. It costs the government money to maintain roads and other public works. Poor folks may pass through only three times a month, whereas the rich come through thirty times. If the toll is raised, the country will have more money to subsidize the poor. The same principle applies to tuition."

This seemingly logical argument drew the following rebuke from the Master: "Rotted wood cannot be carved; a wall made of dung and dirt cannot be plastered over!" What he meant was that a shabby student is not worth teaching. Hearing this, Ziwo felt wronged and said defensively, "It's not that I'm in favor of collecting more tuition; I just want to do some good for the poor."

Confucius' principle of equal educational opportunities for all is encapsulated by the phrase 有教无类 yǒu jiào wú lèi, which is generally interpreted as "When it comes to education, there should be no discrimination." But some scholars have proposed an alternative interpretation that education has an equalizing effect on people. That is, the boundaries that separate people of different social statuses, levels of wealth, intellect, ethnicity and so on will no longer exist once people are educated.

孔子与弟子们回到老家鲁国的时候，发现鲁国士兵在边界关卡收取行人的过路费。孔子很懊恼，更因为付不起所有弟子的过路费而尴尬。这时，一个叫子贡的弟子大方地为大家付了过路费。另一个叫子我的弟子认为这是一个跟老师理论的良机，于是就对孔子说："我早就跟您说过应该涨学费。您管学生吃，管他们住，就是在补贴他们。您收的学费那么低，就等于让有钱的学生搭了便车。要是您涨一点儿学费，就有钱补贴那些真正穷的学生了。就像这个关卡，我觉得国家应该涨过路费。国家维修道路和其他公共设施都是要花钱的。穷人可能一个月只过三次这个关卡，而富人或许来往三十次。要是提高过路费，国家就有钱补贴穷人了。涨学费也是一样的道理。"

这个听起来好像有逻辑的说法遭到了老师一顿训斥，"朽木不可雕也，粪土之墙不可圬也！"孔子的意思就是，一个卑劣的学生是不值得教的。听到师傅这样说，子我委屈地说，"我不是主张多收学费，而是想为穷人办好事啊。"

孔子提倡的人人都应该有平等受教育的机会，就是我们今天说的"有教无类"。然而，一些学者就这个成语提出了另一个解释，就是教育使人们变得平等。换句话说，无论人们来自哪个社会阶层，有多少财富，知识水平怎么样，是什么种族等等，只要接受了教育，他们之间的界限就会消失。

While Confucius was egalitarian in accepting students, he set a very high bar for them. He saw teaching and learning as a two-way process that engaged both the teacher and the student. If a student was unwilling or unable to make inferences from the examples presented by the teacher, then there was no point in teaching them. As the story goes:

> One day Master Confucius said to his students, "I'll raise one corner and if you cannot respond with the other three corners, then I will not repeat myself." In other words, Confucius challenged his students to come up with three new examples from each one he gave to them. If they could not do this, then he will not teach them anymore.

To this day, 举一反三 **jǔ yī fǎn sān** "Raise one return with three" is used to describe the type of students that all teachers love to teach. It also captures the idea that the main job of a teacher is to inspire students to think and learn for themselves, rather than to download knowledge into their brains.

尽管孔子什么学生都愿意教，不过他的标准也很高。在孔子看来，教与学是老师和学生都参与的<u>双向互动</u>。如果学生不愿意或不能从老师给出的例子中作出简单的<u>推理</u>，那教那样的学生是没有意义的。<u>论语</u>里有这么一个故事：

　　有一天，孔子老师跟学生们说："<u>举一隅，不以三隅反，则不复也</u>。"也就是说，孔子要学生们从他举的一个例子推想出其他三个实例。孔子甚至告诉学生们，要是他们做不到，那就不值得他花时间再教他们了。

　　今天，"举一反三"这个成语常用来形容老师们最喜欢教的那类学生。这个成语也表明老师的主要作用就是<u>启发</u>学生，而不是只往学生的脑袋里<u>灌</u>知识。

The Chinese Proverbs

Saying #1:

有	教	无	类
yǒu	**jiào**	**wú**	**lèi**
there is	teaching	there is no	classification/differentiation

Literal meaning: When it comes to teaching there is no segregation.

Connotations:
1. When it comes to education, all students should be treated equally.
2. Once people are educated, differences of class, wealth and origin disappear.

The original source: Chapter "Duke Ling of Wei" in *The Analects of Confucius* (475–221 BCE)《论语·卫灵公》

Saying #2:

举	一	反	三
jǔ	**yī**	**fǎn**	**sān**
raise	one	return	three

Literal meaning: Raise one example and respond with three.

Connotation: Bright students who are able to make their own inferences can take what is taught to them and expand upon it.

The original source: Chapter "Shù Ér" in *The Analects of Confucius* (475–221 BCE) 《论语•述而》

Vocabulary

1. 令   **lìng**   to cause (someone) to...
2. 与···齐名   **yǔ...qímíng**   to be equally famous as...
3. 诞辰   **dànchén**   anniversary of a notable person's birth
4. 感恩   **gǎn'ēn**   to be grateful
5. 惊讶   **jīngyà**   to be surprised
6. 古板   **gǔbǎn**   inflexibly old-fashioned, stuffy
7. 莫测高深   **mò-cè-gāo-shēn**   unfathomable, enigmatic
8. 互动   **hùdòng**   to interact with
9. 弟子   **dìzǐ**   disciple, pupil, follower
10. 周游   **zhōuyóu**   to travel around
11. 鱼龙混杂   **yú-lóng-hùn-zá**   a mixed lot
12. 有心向学   **yǒu xīn xiàng xué**   to be keen on learning
13. 人品   **rénpǐn**   personal character
14. 强盗   **qiángdào**   robber
15. 赞同   **zàntóng**   to endorse
16. 争议   **zhēngyì**   controversy
17. 关卡   **guānqiǎ**   border checkpoint, customs
18. 行人   **xíngrén**   pedestrian, traveler
19. 过路费   **guòlù fèi**   toll, transit fee

20.	懊恼	**àonǎo**	vexed, upset
21.	尴尬	**gāngà**	embarrassed, awkward
22.	跟⋯理论	**gēn...lǐlùn**	to argue with ...
23.	良机	**liángjī**	good opportunity
24.	补贴	**bǔtiē**	to subsidize; subsidy
25.	搭⋯便车	**dā...biànchē**	to hitch a ride
26.	维修	**wéixiū**	to maintain
27.	设施	**shèshī**	facilities
28.	有逻辑	**yǒu luóji**	logical (lit. "to have logic")
29.	遭到	**zāodào**	to incur
30.	训斥	**xùnchì**	reprimand
31.	朽木不可雕也, 粪土之墙不可圬也。	**xiǔmù bùkě diāo yě, fèntǔ zhī qiáng bùkě wū yě**	rotted wood cannot be carved, a wall made of dung and dirt cannot be plastered over
32.	卑劣	**bēiliè**	sordid, despicable
33.	委屈	**wěiqū**	to feel wronged
34.	主张	**zhǔzhāng**	to advocate
35.	提倡	**tíchàng**	to advocate
36.	就⋯	**jiù**	on the subject of ...
37.	界限	**jièxiàn**	boundary
38.	消失	**xiāoshī**	to dissipate, to vanish
39.	双向	**shuāngxiàng**	two-way
40.	推理	**tuīlǐ**	to infer; inference
41.	论语	**Lúnyǔ**	Analects (of Confucius)
42.	举一隅, 不以三隅反, 则不复也。	**jǔ yì yú, bù yǐ sān yú fǎn, zé bú fù yě**	"(I will) raise one corner, (if you) don't respond with three corners, then (I) will not repeat (myself)."
43.	启发	**qǐfā**	to enlighten, to inspire
44.	灌	**guàn**	to pour (into a container)
45.	⋯之际	**...zhī jì**	at the time of ...
46.	封建制	**fēngjiàn-zhì**	feudal system

Need-blind College Admissions

Confucius could never have imagined 2,500 years ago that his philosophy about education would someday be implemented in a world far beyond China. But today most elite colleges in the United States compete to enroll talented students from underprivileged groups and pride themselves on the percentage of ethnic minorities within their student populations. Some institutions even make a special effort to recruit students who are the first in their family to attend college. To match their deeds with their words, these colleges practice "need-blind" admissions. That is, applicants are admitted on the basis of qualifications without regard to their financial status, and all admitted students who need financial assistance will receive financial aid. Of course, "equal opportunities for all students" is a noble ideal, but only the best-endowed institutions can afford it.

....

Discussion questions (discuss in English or Chinese):

1. If you take Ziwo's side in his debate with Master Confucius, what would you say to defend his point of view? Can you think of a solution superior to both points of view?

2. How would you compare Confucius' ideas about education with contemporary principles of education in your country? How do you imagine his ideas were received by his contemporaries?

3. Two other sayings by Confucius are: 1) 三人行，必有我师 **sān rén xíng, bì yǒu wǒ shī**; 2) 学而时习之，不亦乐乎 **xué ér shí xí zhī, bú yì lè hú**? Can you guess what they mean? Look them up and see how close you came to the correct interpretations.

美国优秀贫困生怎么上大学

生活在两千五百年前的孔子一定不会想到他的教育学说有一天会在遥远的海外得到实施。然而，美国的精英院校在招生的时候争相录取来自社会弱势群体的学生，并以少数民族在学生总人数中的高比例为荣。有的大学甚至刻意招收那些家族里的第一代大学生。为了做到言行一致，这些大学实行"无视资金需求"政策，也就是说，学校在录取学生的时候不看他们的经济状况，而录取后对那些经济上有困难的学生发放助学金。"有教无类"固然是一个崇高的理想，但只有基金丰厚的院校才做得到。

Vocabulary

47.	优秀	**yōuxiù**	excellent, outstanding
48.	贫困生	**pínkùn-shēng**	poor (low-income) students
49.	学说	**xuéshuō**	doctrine, philosophy
50.	遥远	**yáoyuǎn**	distant, faraway
51.	实施	**shíshī**	to put into practice, to implement
52.	精英	**jīngyīng**	elite
53.	招生	**zhāoshēng**	to recruit students
54.	争相	**zhēngxiāng**	to vie with each other
55.	录取	**lùqǔ**	to admit (applicants), to enroll
56.	弱势	**ruòshì**	disadvantaged, weak, powerless
57.	群体	**qúntǐ**	group (of people)
58.	以…为荣	**yǐ...wéi róng**	to take pride in ..., to be proud of ...
59.	刻意	**kèyì**	deliberately, intentionally
60.	言行一致	**yán-xíng yízhì**	words and deeds aligned
61.	无视	**wúshì**	to disregard
62.	崇高	**chónggāo**	lofty
63.	基金	**jījīn**	endowment, foundation (financial)
64.	丰厚	**fēnghòu**	wealthy, abundant

The Fox Who Uses the Tiger's Prowess

The fable "The Fox Who Uses the Tiger's Prowess" is familiar to every Chinese person, whether young or old. In this story, the shrewd fox fools the tiger and bullies the smaller animals.

Once upon a time a tiger who lived on a mountain became hungry and searched in the woods for something to eat. He soon came upon a fox and in one leap grabbed it in his claws. As he opened his jaws and was about to sink his teeth into the fox, the fox declared, "Humph! So you think you can eat me just because you are king of the beasts? Well, I am the king of kings sent down by the Lord of Heaven. Whoever eats me will be punished!" On hearing this, the tiger didn't know whether he should believe it, but seeing the fox speak with such authority, he became a bit worried that he would be punished by the Lord of Heaven if he ate the fox. Meanwhile, on seeing the tiger's hesitation, the fox knew that his ruse was succeeding. So he puffed himself up even further and said, "Why, you don't believe me? Just follow me and watch everybody run for their lives when they see me coming." This sounded logical to the tiger, so he agreed. "OK, I'll go with you and see what happens."

So the fox strutted ahead with bold steps while the tiger tip-toed behind him. As they walked through the woods, all the smaller animals ran for their lives when they saw the tiger approaching. Thereupon, the fox turned and said to the tiger smugly, "See? Didn't I tell you?" By this time the tiger was totally convinced, but he had no idea that the little animals were actually afraid of him and that the fox was using him to frighten them.

狐假虎威

"狐假虎威"是一个所有中国人从小就<u>熟悉</u>的童话故事。在这个故事里，<u>狡猾</u>的狐狸<u>欺骗</u>了老虎，并<u>欺负</u>了别的小动物。

从前有一座山上有一只老虎。有一天，老虎饿了，就到林子里找东西吃。走着走着，老虎看见一只狐狸，就一下子扑上去把狐狸抓住了。老虎张开大嘴，正要把狐狸吃下去的时候，狐狸突然说话了："哼，你不要以为自己是<u>百兽之王</u>，就可以吃我。你小心一点，因为我是<u>天帝</u>派来的<u>王中之王</u>。无论谁吃了我，都会<u>遭到</u>天帝的<u>惩罚</u>！"老虎听了狐狸的话，<u>半信半疑</u>，可是看到狐狸一副<u>神气活现</u>的样子，又担心自己吃了狐狸真的会遭到天帝的惩罚。狐狸看见老虎<u>犹豫不决</u>的样子，就知道自己的<u>计谋</u>成功了一半了。于是，狐狸就更神气地说："怎么，难道你还不相信我说的话吗？那你现在跟在我后面，看看大家是不是一看见我就吓得<u>逃之夭夭</u>了。"老虎觉得这主意不错，就跟狐狸说："好吧，那我跟你去看看吧。"

于是，狐狸在前面<u>大摇大摆</u>地走着，老虎在后面<u>小心翼翼</u>地跟着。走进树林里以后，很多小动物看见老虎来了，都吓得<u>飞奔</u>而逃。这时，狐狸回头看着老虎，很得意地说："怎么样，我说的没错吧？"老虎这时就<u>信以为真</u>了，根本不知道那些小动物其实怕的是自己，狐狸只是借着他的威风来<u>吓唬</u>那些小动物。

This fable is not just a clever story for children, because behind it lies a true story of devious infighting among top officials in ancient China. During the Warring States period (ca. 475–221 BCE) over a hundred major and minor feudal states were gradually consolidating through annexation and conquest. By 340 BCE only seven remained. Among these the State of Chu in the South was the most powerful.* While Chu was vying for hegemony against the other powerful states, officials serving King Xuan of Chu competed against one another to gain his favor. Our story involves two of these officials in particular. One by the name of Zhao Xixu was Prime Minister and held the highest military and political position under the king. For his outstanding military service, the king bestowed upon him the fiefdom of Jiang. The other high official, named Jiang Yi, was a clever strategist and skillful schemer who saw Zhao Xixu as his archrival. Jiang Yi took every opportunity to badmouth Zhao Xixu in front of the king, but because the king favored Zhao Xixu, he had to devise cunning tricks to convey his messages.†

For example, Jiang Yi once told this story to the king: "There was once a man who owned a very fierce dog. One day, the dog peed in the owner's well. This dastardly act caught the eye of a neighbor who tried to report it to the dog's owner. But the fierce dog blocked the doorway so the neighbor could not get through to the owner." In telling this story, Jiang Yi meant to tip off King Xuan that Zhao Xixu, like that fierce dog, had unfairly set up barriers to block other officials from seeing the king, so they had no way to present their good advice and suggestions to him. Obviously, Jiang Yi was hoping to discredit Zhao Xixu in the king's eyes.

---

* Eventually, in 221 BCE, the First Emperor of Qin conquered the other six feudal states and united China, thus founding the first imperial dynasty in Chinese history.

† It is natural for important officials in a court to be rivals. But Jiang Yi may have had a special reason to be especially resentful of Zhao Xixu. The feudal state to which Jiang Yi's ancestors belonged was conquered by the State of Chu almost 300 years before this time, and that feudal state was exactly the region that King Xuan of Chu bestowed on Zhao Xixu.

这个生动的童话故事背后实际上有一段宫廷大臣之间明争暗斗的历史。战国时代（公元前475-221年），一百多个大大小小的诸侯国经过多年征战，在公元前340年左右形成了七个国家，而南方楚国的势力达到了强盛时期。*就在楚国与其他诸侯国争霸的时候，宫廷里的大臣们也在为得到楚宣王的宠幸而互相争斗。其中有两位大臣，一位叫昭奚恤，是楚国当时的令尹，也就是楚宣王之下地位最高的军政大臣。因为昭奚恤战功显赫，楚宣王册封他为江君。另一位大臣叫江乙，善谋而有心机。江乙把昭奚恤看成死对头，因此常在楚宣王面前说昭奚恤的坏话。可是因为楚宣王宠爱昭奚恤，江乙就得想一些诡计来说服楚宣王。†

有一次，江乙对楚宣王说："有个人有一条很厉害的狗。有一天狗往井里撒尿，被邻居看见了。邻居要告诉狗的主人，可是狗很凶，挡住了门，所以邻居没见到主人。"江乙讲这个故事是向楚宣王暗示，昭奚恤就是那条很凶的狗，想方设法阻止他和别的大臣见到楚宣王，不让他们给楚宣王献计献策。可见江乙的目的就是希望昭奚恤在楚宣王面前失宠。

---

* 公元前221年，秦始皇征服了其他六个诸侯国，统一了中国，建立了中国历史上第一个皇朝。

† 在宫廷里，重臣之间互相争斗是很自然的。但江乙忌恨昭奚恤可能有这样一个原因：江乙的祖先所属的诸侯国在楚宣王前近300年被楚国所灭，而那片土地后来册封给了昭奚恤。

On another occasion, the king asked all the high officials, "I have heard that all the states to the North are intimidated by Zhao Xixu. How could that be?" None of the officials knew what to say except for Jiang Yi, who immediately saw a golden opportunity to denigrate Zhao Xixu before the king. So he told the story about the fox who exploited the tiger's prowess, then concluded the story with this comment: "Great King, in truth the reason why all the states to the North fear Zhao Xixu is because he holds the king's military power in his hands. What they fear is actually not Zhao Xixu but you, great King!"

The above story ends without telling us what immediate effect the story about the fox exploiting the tiger's prowess had on the king, but eventually the king did reduce the power placed in Zhao's hand. It is not clear from historical records whether either Zhao Xixu or Jiang Yi was actually evil or disloyal. What is obvious is that there was treacherous infighting within the court.

还有一次，楚宣王问所有的大臣："听说北方各国都很惧怕昭奚恤，这是为什么呢？"别的大臣都不知道怎么回答，江乙马上意识到这是在楚宣王面前贬损昭奚恤的绝好机会，于是就讲了"狐假虎威"的故事。最后，江乙说到了故事的重点："大王啊，其实北方各国之所以惧怕昭奚恤，是因为他掌握着大王的兵权，其实他们害怕的并不是昭奚恤，而是大王您啊。"

这个故事没告诉我们楚宣王听了狐假虎威的故事之后有什么反应，但楚宣王后来确实削弱了昭奚恤手中的权力。历史资料对昭奚恤和江乙是忠臣还是奸臣并没有十分清楚的评价，但是宫廷里大臣之间的明争暗斗是显而易见的。

The Chinese Proverb

狐	假	虎	威
hú	**jiǎ**	**hǔ**	**wēi**
fox	to fake, expropriate	tiger	awesomeness, prowess

Literal meaning: The fox expropriated the tiger's prowess.

Connotation: A devious person who exploits his or her connections to a powerful person to bully others.

The original source: "Stratagems of Chu, Part I", a chapter in *Stratagems of the Warring States*. Collated an edited by Liu Xiang (77–6 BCE, Han dynasty) 《战国策•楚策一》汉朝刘向编订

Vocabulary

1.	熟悉	shúxī	to know something well, to be familiar with
2.	狡猾	jiǎohuá	sly, cunning
3.	欺骗	qīpiàn	to cheat, to swindle
4.	欺负	qīfu	to bully, to browbeat
5.	百兽之王	bǎi shòu zhī wáng	king of all the beasts
6.	天帝	tiāndì	Lord of Heaven
7.	王中之王	wáng zhōng zhī wáng	king among kings
8.	遭到	zāodào	to incur
9.	惩罚	chéngfá	to punish
10.	半信半疑	bàn xìn bàn yí	half-believing, half-doubting
11.	神气活现	shénqi huóxiàn	very cocky, full of bravado
12.	犹豫不决	yóuyù bùjué	hesitant and unable to decide
13.	计谋	jìmóu	scheme, stratagem
14.	逃之夭夭	táo zhī yāoyāo	to flee and disappear
15.	大摇大摆	dàyáo dàbǎi	to swagger, to strut
16.	小心翼翼	xiǎoxīn yìyì	very cautiously
17.	飞奔	fēibēn	run with flying speed
18.	信以为真	xìn yǐ wéi zhēn	to take as real
19.	吓唬	xiàhu	to threaten, to frighten
20.	宫廷	gōngtíng	court (of a king)
21.	大臣	dàchén	top officials
22.	明争暗斗	míngzhēng àndòu	open strife and veiled struggle
23.	诸侯国	zhūhóu-guó	feudal states
24.	征战	zhēngzhàn	conquest and war
25.	势力	shìlì	power, influence
26.	强盛	qiángshèng	strong and prosperous
27.	争霸	zhēngbà	to vie for hegemony
28.	宠幸	chǒngxìng	to favor (someone)
29.	争斗	zhēngdòu	to fight, to struggle
30.	令尹	lìngyǐn	highest official in ancient China (equivalent to today's prime minister)
31.	军政	jūn zhèng	military and political
32.	战功显赫	zhàngōng xiǎnhè	military feats being superb
33.	册封	cèfēng	to confer title/land (to a noble)

34.	江君	**Jiāng Jūn**	Lord of Jiang
35.	善谋	**shànmóu**	skilled at strategizing
36.	心机	**xīnjī**	scheming
37.	死对头	**sǐ duìtóu**	dead rival
38.	宠爱	**chǒng'ài**	to favor (someone), to dote on
39.	诡计	**guǐjì**	ruse, trick
40.	说服	**shuōfú**	to convince
41.	井	**jǐng**	a well
42.	撒尿	**sā niào**	to urinate
43.	邻居	**línjū**	neighbor
44.	凶	**xiōng**	fierce
45.	挡住	**dǎngzhù**	to block
46.	暗示	**ànshì**	to hint
47.	想方设法	**xiǎngfāng shèfǎ**	to think of all kinds of ways
48.	阻止	**zǔzhǐ**	to obstruct, to prevent
49.	献计献策	**xiànjì xiàncè**	to propose various strategies
50.	失宠	**shī chǒng**	to lose favor
51.	惧怕	**jùpà**	to fear
52.	意识到	**yìshi dào**	to become aware of
53.	贬损	**biǎnsǔn**	to denigrate
54.	之所以… 是因为…	**zhīsuǒyǐ...shì yīnwèi...**	the reason why...is that...
55.	掌握	**zhǎngwò**	to grasp, to hold in one's hand
56.	兵权	**bīngquán**	military power
57.	反应	**fǎnyìng**	reaction
58.	削弱	**xuēruò**	to weaken
59.	资料	**zīliào**	data, material
60.	忠臣	**zhōng chén**	loyal court official
61.	奸臣	**jiān chén**	treacherous court official
62.	评价	**píngjià**	evaluation, assessment
63.	显而易见	**xiǎn ér yì jiàn**	obvious and easy to see
64.	征服	**zhēngfú**	to conquer
65.	皇朝	**huángcháo**	imperial dynasty
66.	忌恨	**jìhèn**	to resent, to envy
67.	所属	**suǒ shú**	to belong to...
68.	灭	**miè**	to extinguish, to annihilate

Madame Mao: A Paper Tiger

The saying "the fox who exploits the tiger's prowess" has been applied to Mao Zedong's fourth and final wife Jiang Qing by many historians. Her ascent to political power would not have been possible without Mao's power and prestige. This relationship between Mao and Jiang Qing reached its most obvious point in the final years of the Cultural Revolution, when Mao's health had greatly deteriorated and the Gang of Four led by Jiang Qing held absolute power. The fall of Jiang Qing and the Gang of Four came less than a month after Mao's death, which further confirms that without Mao's backing, Jiang Qing was nothing but a paper tiger.

Discussion questions (discuss in English or Chinese):

1. Can you think of a military or political situation in the West to which the saying "the fox who exploits the tiger's prowess" can be applied? How about the relationship between Henry Kissinger and Richard Nixon?

2. Have you heard of the beloved character Gruffalo? It is from a story about a clever little mouse who invented a fantastical creature called Gruffalo to scare off all the other animals in the forest that preyed on him. Can you imagine the similarities and differences between the story of the Gruffalo and the story of the fox that exploited the tiger's prowess?

3. Have you ever encountered a situation in your life that is an example of the tactic shown in "the fox who exploits the tiger's prowess"? What kind of social environment is likely to spawn this type of situation?

4. If you have observed a case of "a fox exploiting the tiger's prowess," what was the relationship between the fox and the tiger? And what was the final outcome of that relationship?

毛主席的妻子江青

许多历史学家都曾经用狐假虎威这个成语来形容毛泽东的第四任，也是最后一任妻子江青。要不是因为毛泽东的地位与威望，江青不可能在政治上有那么大的权力。在文化大革命的后期，毛泽东的健康状况恶化以后，四人帮实际上控制了整个局面，江青更是充分利用了她第一夫人的身份。毛泽东去世后不到一个月，江青和四人帮就倒台了。这进一步说明，没有毛泽东的话，江青就是一只纸老虎。

Vocabulary

69.	威望	**wēiwàng**	prestige
70.	恶化	**èhuà**	to deteriorate
71.	四人帮	**Sìrénbāng**	Gang of Four
72.	局面	**júmiàn**	situation, aspect
73.	身份	**shēnfèn**	status, identity
74.	倒台	**dǎotái**	to fall from power

Trust Old Horses to Know the Way

Many cultures in the ancient world had a knowledge of the superior sense of direction of horses. Some cultures made good use of this wisdom, but it was the Chinese who immortalized it in a proverb.

During the Spring and Autumn period (770–476 BCE), feudal states in China's heartland were under the titular rule of the Zhou dynasty, although they were beginning to assert their autonomy and engage in infighting. King Huan of Qi (reigned 685–643 BCE) was recognized as a benevolent elder brother by the other states. In 679 BCE, he convened a United Nations-like conference wherein all the states pledged to support the weaker members and defend them against foreign invasions.

At this time, one of the northern states—Yan—was plagued by raids from non-Chinese nomadic people from the north called the Shanrong. These people, who were from various tribes, frequently raided the northern states in the alliance for grain, livestock and other valuables, even abducting women and able-bodied men. In 663 BCE, Yan was again attacked by the Shanrong and sought aid from King Huan of Qi. True to his word, King Huan mounted a military campaign with the intention of eradicating the rogue Shanrong tribes once and for all. But by the time his army reached the state of Yan, the Shanrong had fled further north.

Although King Huan wanted to pursue them, his army had one serious handicap—they were unfamiliar with the terrain. The King of Yan however informed King Huan that the neighboring state of Wuzhong was originally a Shanrong tribe but now no longer allied themselves with the Shanrong, so they could be asked to act as guides. Thus the armies of Qi, Yan and Wuzhong joined forces and together gave chase to the Shanrong, who fled to the Shanrong territory of Guzhu.

Guzhu had an extremely wily and treacherous general by the name of Yellow Flower who managed to trick King Huan into believing that he was surrendering and switching his allegiance to the king. He did this by beheading the chief of another Shanrong tribe and presenting the head to King Huan. Moreover, he declared that he was ready to help King Huan

老马识途

从古代起，世界各地就已经有人认识到马具有超人的方向感，并且很好地利用了这种知识。马的这个特点在中国文化里更是通过一个成语故事而流传千古。

春秋时代（公元前770-476年），虽然中原大地上的诸侯国名义上还在周王朝的统治之下，但诸侯之间实际上已经开始相互割据争霸。当时，齐桓公（公元前685-643年在位）是诸侯各国公认的一位仁慈的老大哥。公元前679年，齐桓公召集各诸侯会盟。就像在今天的联合国安理会一样，诸侯各国都宣誓帮助弱小的诸侯，共同抵御外族入侵。

那个时候，北方的诸侯国，尤其是燕国，常常受到来自北方山戎游牧民族的骚扰。这些山戎包括不同的部落，经常侵犯北方诸侯国，抢夺粮食，牲畜和财物，有时候甚至劫持良家妇女和壮丁。公元前663年，山戎又一次侵犯燕国，所以燕国就请求齐桓公出兵攻打山戎。齐桓公亲自带领大军出征北方，打算彻底消灭山戎。齐桓公的军队到了燕国的时候，山戎已经逃往北方去了。

对齐桓公来说，一个不利的因素是他们的军队不熟悉北方的地形。燕王就告诉齐桓公邻近的无终国原来也是一个山戎部落，但是已不依附山戎，可以请他们做向导。于是，齐军，燕军和无终国军就联合起来，一路往北追杀逃跑到孤竹国去的山戎了。

孤竹国有一个十分狡诈的将领，名叫黄花。为了让齐桓公相信他要投降，并效忠于齐国，黄花杀了山戎部落的一个头领，提着他的头颅去见了齐桓公，谎称要帮助齐桓公抓捕

capture the chief of Guzhu. King Huan was delighted and he followed Yellow Flower into a forbidding desert called Lost Valley. It was said that no outsider who ventured into this territory ever came out alive. Sure enough, soon after King Huan's troops entered Lost Valley, they became totally lost, and Yellow Flower and his troops were nowhere to be found. At this critical moment, the wise minister Guan Zhong remembered that some of the horses were from the former Shanrong state of Wuzhong, and he surmised that these horses knew the terrain. So he proposed to King Huan that they let these horses lead the way. Much to everyone's surprise, the Wuzhang horses soon led them out of Lost Valley.

Having escaped from Lost Valley, King Huan and his troops quickly attacked the state of Guzhu. The chief of Guzhu and his general Yellow Flower never imagined that King Huan's troops would emerge alive from that death trap. In the end, the chief was captured and beheaded at King Huan's own hands, and Yellow Flower died in battle. The Shanrong threat was totally eliminated by 660 BCE.

孤竹国的头领。齐桓公很高兴，就带着军队跟着黄花进了一个叫做"迷谷"的地方。据说，误入迷谷的人从来没有活着出去的。齐国军队在茫茫的迷谷里走了一会儿就彻底迷路了，而黄花早就带着自己的人逃跑了。在这个关键时刻，聪明的宰相管仲想起来军队里有一些从无终国来的马应该了解这里的地形，所以就建议齐桓公让那些马来带路。果然，没过多久，这些马就把大军带出了迷谷。

走出迷谷的齐国大军追杀到孤竹国。孤竹国头领和黄花怎么都没有想到齐国军队能从迷谷里死里逃生。最后，孤竹国头领被抓，齐桓公亲自砍了他的头，而黄花也战死了。山戎最终在公元前660年被彻底消灭了。

The Chinese Proverb

老	马	识	途
lǎo	**mǎ**	**shí**	**tú**
old	horse	to know	the path

Literal meaning: Old horses know the way.

Connotation: Elderly people should be respected for their experience. Regardless of their current position, their experience is valuable, even critical, in certain circumstances such as an emergency. People who are in charge should seek the guidance of such "old horses."

The original source: Chapter 21, "Guan Zhong's Astute Perception, and How King Huan of Qi Subdued the State of Guzhu," *Annals of the Various States of the Eastern Zhou Dynasty*, a historical novel by Feng Menglong (1574–1646, Ming dynasty). 《东周列国志》第二十一回　管夷吾智辨俞儿　齐桓公兵定孤竹。明朝冯梦龙 (1574–1646) 所著长篇历史小说。

Vocabulary

1.	具有	jùyǒu	to possess
2.	超人	chāorén	superhuman
3.	方向感	fāngxiànggǎn	sense of direction
4.	利用	lìyòng	to make use of, to take advantage of
5.	流传千古	liúchuán qiāngǔ	to pass down through the ages
6.	中原	Zhōngyuán	central plains (China's heartland)
7.	诸侯国	zhūhóu-guó	feudal states (诸侯 zhūhóu: feudal lord)
8.	名义上	míngyìshang	in name (implying not in reality), nominally
9.	周王朝	Zhōu wángcháo	Zhou dynasty
10.	统治	tǒngzhì	to rule
11.	割据	gējù	to set up separate regimes
12.	争霸	zhēngbà	to vie for hegemony
13.	在位	zàiwèi	to reign
14.	公认	gōngrèn	to be publicly recognized

15.	仁慈	réncí	benevolent
16.	召集	zhāojí	to convene
17.	会盟	huìméng	summit meeting of allies
18.	联合国安理会	Liánhéguó Ānlǐhuì	United Nations Security Council
19.	宣誓	xuānshì	to pledge
20.	弱小	ruòxiǎo	weak and small
21.	抵御	dǐyù	to defend against
22.	入侵	rùqīn	incursion
23.	山戎	Shānróng	name of a nomadic people (literally "mountain militants")
24.	游牧民族	yóumù mínzú	nomadic peoples
25.	骚扰	sāorǎo	to harass
26.	部落	bùluò	tribe
27.	侵犯	qīnfàn	to encroach on
28.	抢夺	qiǎngduó	to snatch, to seize
29.	粮食	liángshi	grain
30.	牲畜	shēngchù	livestock
31.	财物	cáiwù	valuable goods
32.	劫持	jiéchí	to abduct
33.	良家妇女	liángjiā fùnǚ	women from good families
34.	壮丁	zhuàngdīng	able-bodied men
35.	出兵攻打	chūbīng gōngdǎ	to dispatch troops to attack
36.	亲自	qīnzì	to personally (do something)
37.	出征	chūzhēng	to go on a military expedition, to go into battle
38.	彻底	chèdǐ	thoroughly, once and for all
39.	消灭	xiāomiè	to eradicate
40.	不利	búlì	disadvantageous
41.	因素	yīnsù	element, factor
42.	熟悉	shúxī	to be familiar with
43.	地形	dìxíng	terrain

44. 邻近	línjìn	neighboring, nearby
45. 依附	yīfù	to depend on, to attach oneself to
46. 向导	xiàngdǎo	to act as a guide
47. 追杀	zhuīshā	to chase and kill
48. 狡诈	jiǎozhà	deceitful, cunning
49. 将领	jiànglǐng	(military) general
50. 投降	tóuxiáng	to surrender
51. 效忠于	xiàozhōng yú	to pledge loyalty to
52. 头领	tóulǐng	chief, leader
53. 头颅	tóulú	head, skull
54. 谎称	huǎngchēng	to falsely allege
55. 抓捕	zhuābǔ	to capture

China Calls Back an "Old Horse Who Knows the Way" for US-China Trade Talks

In recent years, trade between U.S. and China—the two largest economies in the world today—grew exponentially and their economies became increasingly intertwined. Concurrently, trade friction between the two nations has also intensified. After Trump became the U.S. president in 2017, the U.S. veered toward an increasingly hard line on trade issues with China, forcing the two nations to engage in prolonged and arduous negotiations. Before long, the persistent disputes pitched the negotiations into a deadlock. In April of 2019, Yu Jianhua, China's ambassador to the United Nations' offices in Geneva, was called back to Beijing to join the Chinese team in U.S.–China trade talks. Ambassador Yu, a 28-year veteran of trade talks with American officials and at the World Trade Organization, has a stellar track record of dealing with the U.S. and is widely recognized as one of China's most formidable trade negotiators. With his participation, a small breakthrough in the deadlock took place, and in January of 2020, the two sides were finally brought together to sign the first phase of a trade agreement.

56.	迷谷	**Mígǔ**	Lost Valley
57.	误入	**wùrù**	to enter by mistake
58.	茫茫	**mángmáng**	vast and indistinct
59.	迷路	**mílù**	to be lost, to lose one's way
60.	关键时刻	**guānjiàn shíkè**	critical moment
61.	宰相	**zǎixiàng**	prime minister
62.	建议	**jiànyì**	to suggest, to propose
63.	带路	**dàilù**	to lead the way
64.	果然	**guǒrán**	sure enough
65.	死里逃生	**sǐlǐ táoshēng**	to escape death and come out alive
66.	抓	**zhuā**	to capture
67.	砍头	**kǎntóu**	to behead (lit. "to chop the head off")

....

成语今用实例

识途的老马加入中美贸易谈判

作为当今世界上最大的两个经济体, 中美两国在经济贸易上的往来不断加深, 贸易规模也日益扩大, 而两国间的贸易摩擦也在加剧。特朗普在2017年当上美国总统后, 在中美贸易问题上采取了更加强硬的态度, 中美双方随之展开了漫长而艰巨的谈判。双方在一些问题上存在的分歧使谈判陷入僵局。2019年4月, 中国驻联合国日内瓦办事处大使俞建华被调回了北京, 加入了中美贸易谈判中方团队。据报道, 俞建华与美国官员和世界贸易组织进行过28年的贸易谈判, 被认为是"最令人生畏"并"与美国打过交道的最精明的中国贸易官员之一。"随后, 中美贸易谈判出现了突破。在2020年1月, 双方终于签署了第一阶段的经贸协议。

Vocabulary

68.	贸易	**màoyì**	trade, commerce
69.	谈判	**tánpàn**	negotiation
70.	经济体	**jīngjìtǐ**	economic entity, economy
71.	往来	**wǎnglái**	contact, intercourse
72.	规模	**guīmó**	scale, scope
73.	日益	**rìyì**	increasing day by day, increasingly
74.	摩擦	**mócā**	friction
75.	加剧	**jiājù**	to intensify
76.	特朗普	**Tèlǎngpǔ**	Trump
77.	采取	**cǎiqǔ**	to adopt
78.	强硬	**qiángyìng**	tough, unyielding
79.	随之	**suízhī**	following from that
80.	漫长	**màncháng**	prolonged
81.	艰巨	**jiānjù**	arduous
82.	分歧	**fēnqí**	disagreement, difference in opinion
83.	陷入	**xiànrù**	to fall into, to be mired in
84.	僵局	**jiāngjú**	stalemate, deadlock
85.	驻	**zhù**	to be posted to, to be stationed at
86.	日内瓦	**Rìnèiwǎ**	Geneva
87.	大使	**dàshǐ**	ambassador
88.	团队	**tuánduì**	team
89.	世界贸易组织	**Shìjiè Màoyì Zǔzhī**	World Trade Organization (WTO)
90.	令人生畏	**lìngrén shēngwèi**	intimidating, awe-inspiring
91.	打⋯交道	**dǎ...jiāodào**	to have dealings with…, to interact with…
92.	精明	**jīngmíng**	astute, sagacious
93.	突破	**tūpò**	breakthrough
94.	签署	**qiānshǔ**	to sign (a document)
95.	阶段	**jiēduàn**	phase, stage
96.	协议	**xiéyì**	agreement

Discussion questions (discuss in English or Chinese):

1. Have you or your team ever been caught in a predicament and sought the help of an experienced person who had been long retired? What was the outcome? Did the "old horse" still know the way?

2. Now that we have access to the infinite memory of computers and artificial intelligence, isn't the idea of "trusting the old horses to know the way" obsolete?

3. Humans are supposedly the most intelligent creatures on earth, so why is it that we rely on records, maps, and GPS to find our way, while other creatures in the animal kingdom, especially those that migrate seasonally, are able to find their way instinctively?

Waiting for Rabbits by a Tree Stump

Over 2,000 years ago in the ancient state of Song, there was a hardworking farmer who toiled from morning until night. Every day he was out working in the field before any of his neighbors, and he didn't quit until after everyone else had gone home. In a good year, he grew the best crops in his village and everyone envied him. But in a year when they were hit with drought or flood, the harvest would barely be enough to get through the winter and his family suffered like everyone else. He wished there was a better way to ensure there would be enough food on the table for his family, but he couldn't think of any bright ideas, so he just kept on working hard.

Then one day a miracle occurred. The farmer was hoeing his field under the hot sun when he heard a commotion in the distance. He saw a couple of hunters running and yelling. The next thing he saw was a frantic rabbit running for its life. A split second later, he saw the rabbit dash into a tree stump. The poor creature broke its neck, whimpered for a few seconds, then went totally limp.

When the farmer got over his shock, a happy thought came to him: "Wow! I got this rabbit just by standing here near the stump. The rabbit will be a real treat for my family, and I can even sell the rabbit fur for a bit of cash. If I can catch one rabbit each day this way, I'll be rich and I won't have to toil under the hot sun anymore!"

From that day on, the farmer abandoned his hoe and sat under a tree near the stump waiting for another rabbit to appear. He waited and waited, until his field was covered with weeds. As far as we know, no rabbit ever dashed itself against that stump again. When word got around, the farmer became a laughingstock throughout the state of Song.

In Chinese culture, the phrase "waiting for rabbits by a tree stump" has become a colorful way to express the idea that we shouldn't expect the same miracle to happen twice. Just because we had a stroke of luck, we would be foolish to sit around and wait for it to repeat itself. Moreover, only a good-for-nothing would expect to get something without working!

守株待兔

两千多年前，在战国时期的宋国，有一个勤劳的农夫每天早出晚归，在田地里干活。遇到好年景，他种的庄稼是村子里最好的，村民们都很羡慕他。要是遇到旱灾或是涝灾，他家就跟村子里别人家一样，地里的收成只能让一家人勉强填饱肚子，熬过冬天。他最大的愿望就是找到一个更好的办法，来保证家里天天都有足够的食物。然而，除了整天在地里干活以外，他也实在想不出什么好办法。

有一天，奇迹出现了！农夫正在烈日炎炎下的地里干活，听到远处传来喧闹的声音，然后他看见一些打猎的人一边跑一边大声地叫着。这时候，他又看见一只为了逃命而飞奔的野兔。刹那间，那只野兔撞到了一个树桩上。可怜的家伙撞断了脖颈，喘息了片刻，就一动不动了。

农夫看得惊呆了，但很快就喜上心头：天哪，我站在这树桩旁边，就白捡了这只野兔。对家人来说，这可是一顿美餐啊；另外把兔皮卖了还可以赚一点儿钱。要是我每天都这样白捡一只野兔，就可以发财了，而且也不用在大太阳下辛辛苦苦地劳动了。

从那以后，农夫就丢了锄头，整天坐在靠近那个树桩的一棵树下等着下一只野兔的出现。他等了又等，直到地里长满了杂草，也没有再看到另一只野兔撞到那个树桩上。没过多久，农夫就成了宋国的笑柄。

在中国文化里，"守株待兔"这个成语指的就是人们不能期望奇迹重现。幸运降临过一次以后，坐等幸运降临第二次是很愚蠢的。再说了，只有懒虫才会期望不劳而获！

The author of this story—the great legalist philosopher Han Feizi (280–233 BCE)—had an even more serious message in mind. He told this story in the opening passage of a long political treatise on how a ruler should adopt new methods of governance and change the laws to keep up with changing times, rather than sticking with the "tried and true" methods used by other rulers in the past. The story of the foolish farmer waiting for another miracle concludes with this admonition: "Wishing to use the policies of former kings to govern people in contemporary times is just as foolish as waiting for rabbits by a tree stump." It is said that the great emperor of Qin held Han Feizi's philosophy in high regard, and this was one of the critical factors that enabled him to unify China for the first time in Chinese history.

著名的法家大师韩非子（公元前280–233年）写这个故事的时候有更深的寓意。他用"守株待兔"作为其长篇政论文的开篇，论述一国之君必须随着时代的变化而采用新的治国方法和改变法律，而不是一直沿袭过去的君王老一套的成功经验。在这个寓言故事之后，韩非子加了这么一句结语："如果一个君王想用先王的政策来治理当代的民众，那就跟守株待兔的那个农夫一样愚蠢了。"据说，秦始皇很推崇韩非子的学说，而这正是他能够统一全中国，成为中国历史上始皇帝的一个重要因素。

The Chinese Proverb

守	株	待	兔
shǒu	**zhū**	**dài**	**tù**
keep watch	a tree stump	to wait for	a rabbit

Literal meaning: Keeping watch by a tree stump waiting for rabbits.

Connotation: It is foolish to wait for a stroke of luck to happen again just because it happened once before. It is impractical to stick with a way of doing something just because it worked once in the past.

The original source: The Five Vermin, a political treatise by Han Feizi (280–233 BCE), Warring States period.《五蠹》，战国时期·韩非子（公元前280–233年）著。

Vocabulary

1.	勤劳	**qínláo**	diligent, hardworking
2.	农夫	**nóngfū**	farmer
3.	早出晚归	**zǎo chū wǎn guī**	start out early and return late
4.	干活	**gànhuó**	to do work (colloquial)
5.	好年景	**hǎo niánjǐng**	good year, good harvest (colloquial)
6.	庄稼	**zhuāngjia**	crops
7.	羡慕	**xiànmù**	to admire, to envy
8.	旱灾	**hànzāi**	drought disaster
9.	涝灾	**làozāi**	crop failure due to flooding
10.	收成	**shōuchéng**	harvest
11.	勉强	**miǎnqiǎng**	straining to do something; to do with difficulty
12.	填饱	**tiánbǎo**	to fill (one's belly)
13.	熬过	**áoguò**	to get through (a hardship)
14.	保证	**bǎozhèng**	to guarantee
15.	食物	**shíwù**	food
16.	奇迹	**qíjì**	miracle
17.	烈日炎炎	**lièrì yányán**	blazing hot sun
18.	喧闹	**xuānnào**	ruckus, bustle
19.	打猎	**dǎliè**	to hunt
20.	逃命	**táomìng**	to run for one's life
21.	飞奔	**fēibēn**	to run at a flying speed
22.	野兔	**yětù**	wild rabbit
23.	刹那间	**chà'nàjiān**	in an instant
24.	撞	**zhuàng**	to crash into
25.	树桩	**shùzhuāng**	tree stump
26.	脖颈	**bójǐng**	neck
27.	喘息	**chuǎnxī**	to gasp for breath
28.	片刻	**piànkè**	a brief moment
29.	一动不动	**yí dòng bú dòng**	motionless
30.	惊呆	**jīngdāi**	stupefied
31.	喜上心头	**xǐ shàng xīntóu**	a happy thought comes to mind
32.	白捡	**bái jiǎn**	to pick up something without any effort (白: for nothing)

33.	美餐	**měicān**	delicious meal
34.	皮	**pí**	skin, fur
35.	发财	**fācái**	to get rich
36.	辛辛苦苦	**xīnxin-kǔkǔ**	taking great pains
37.	锄头	**chútou**	hoe
38.	杂草	**zácǎo**	weeds
39.	笑柄	**xiàobǐng**	laughingstock
40.	期望	**qīwàng**	to expect
41.	重现	**chóngxiàn**	to appear again
42.	降临	**jiànglín**	to arrive, to befall
43.	愚蠢	**yúchǔn**	stupid, foolish
44.	懒虫	**lǎnchóng**	lazy bum
45.	不劳而获	**bù láo ér huò**	to reap without sowing (lit. "no labor but obtain")
46.	法家	**fǎjiā**	Legalist school of thought
47.	大师	**dàshī**	great master
48.	公元前	**gōngyuán qián**	BCE
49.	寓意	**yùyì**	message, moral (or a story), implication
50.	政论文	**zhènglùnwén**	political essay
51.	开篇	**kāipiān**	opening of an essay or book
52.	论述	**lùnshù**	to discuss, to expound
53.	君	**jūn**	ruler, king
54.	采用	**cǎiyòng**	to adopt (a plan, method, etc.)
55.	治国	**zhìguó**	to govern a country
56.	法律	**fǎlǜ**	law
57.	沿袭	**yánxí**	to carry on as before, to follow an old practice
58.	君王	**jūnwáng**	ruler, king
59.	老(一)套	**lǎo(yí)tào**	old way, old stuff
60.	寓言	**yùyán**	fable, parable
61.	结语	**jiéyǔ**	conclusion, concluding remarks
62.	政策	**zhèngcè**	policy
63.	秦始皇	**Qín Shǐ Huáng**	First Emperor of the Qin dynasty
64.	推崇	**tuīchóng**	to hold in high esteem
65.	学说	**xuéshuō**	philosophy, doctrine, theory
66.	因素	**yīnsù**	factor

Waiting at Starbucks for a Mate

My friend Carly is the most wonderful person—vivacious, caring, talented, hardworking, smart and funny—as well as being tall and beautiful. She has had a great career but there was one thing missing: She had a hard time finding a match to be her mate. Carly wasn't too worried about this because she did have some success in the past. Back in graduate school she met her first boyfriend by accident. She was at a Starbucks engrossed in typing a paper, unconsciously swinging her leg. In walked a tall, handsome man who tripped over her swinging leg. That incident started a wonderful four-year relationship. Something similar happened several years later when Carly was working in Hong Kong. So she developed a habit of spending her Saturday mornings in coffee shops, working on her laptop. She accomplished quite a lot on her laptop but never again met anyone interesting.

One day, she found out that several of her friends had joined a dating website. Then it dawned on her that she had been stuck in her romantic dreams, "waiting for another rabbit by a tree stump." She realized that in these modern times, a lady needs to be proactive and strategic and not wait for fate to deliver to her the man of her dreams. We don't know if Carly joined a dating website herself but she did abandon her "stump," and in less than a year she married the love of her life. One year later they became the happy parents of a beautiful baby!

找对象

我的朋友卡莉是个优秀的女士：活泼可爱，充满爱心，多才多艺，努力向上，聪明俏皮，而且长得又高又漂亮。卡莉事业有成，但个人生活中有一个遗憾，就是找不到一个配得上她的伴侣。卡莉并不太着急，因为她有过成功的经验。卡莉上研究所的时候偶然遇到了她的第一个男朋友。有一天，她带着电脑，在一家星巴克里全神贯注地写着文章，无意识地摇晃着一条腿。这时候，走进来一个高大英俊的帅哥。卡莉的腿绊倒了帅哥，于是两人开始了长达四年的恋情。几年后，卡莉在香港工作期间又发生了一次类似的故事。因此，卡莉养成了一个习惯，每周六上午带着电脑去不同的咖啡馆作些事情。她在电脑上完成了许多事情，可是再也没有碰到有意思的帅哥了。

有一天，卡莉发现她的几个好友都在一个约会网站上找对象，她这才恍然大悟，原来自己一直沉迷在罗曼蒂克的梦想当中，守株等待着下一只野兔！卡莉意识到，在现代化的今天，淑女也得积极主动，并且要有策略，而不是被动地等待着命运给她带来梦想中的对象。我们不知道卡莉有没有加入一个约会网站，不过她肯定不再守着那个"树桩"了。不到一年的时间，她就找到了真爱。一年之后，两人就有了一个美丽小宝宝，成为了快乐的父母亲！

Vocabulary

67.	对象	**duìxiàng**	boyfriend/girlfriend, potential spouse
68.	优秀	**yōuxiù**	outstanding
69.	活泼	**huópo**	lively, vivacious
70.	多才多艺	**duō cái duō yì**	multi-talented
71.	俏皮	**qiàopí**	witty, lively
72.	事业有成	**shìyè yǒuchéng**	professionally accomplished
73.	遗憾	**yíhàn**	a regret, a pity
74.	配得上	**pèideshàng**	able to match, up to...
75.	伴侣	**bànlǚ**	mate, partner
76.	研究所	**yánjiūsuǒ**	graduate school
77.	偶然	**ǒurán**	by chance
78.	星巴克	**Xīngbākè**	Starbucks
79.	全神贯注	**quánshén guànzhù**	totally focused
80.	无意识	**wúyìshí**	unconsciously
81.	摇晃	**yáohuang**	to sway, to rock
82.	英俊	**yīngjùn**	handsome
83.	帅哥	**shuàigē**	handsome man (colloquial)
84.	绊倒	**bàndǎo**	to trip over, to stumble
85.	长达	**chángdá**	to extend to a period of ..., to last
86.	恋情	**liànqíng**	love affair
87.	类似	**lèisì**	similar
88.	约会网站	**yuēhuì wǎngzhàn**	dating website
89.	恍然大悟	**huǎngrán dàwù**	to have a sudden realization
90.	沉迷	**chénmí**	bewitched (by some fantasy)
91.	罗曼蒂克	**luómàndìkè**	romantic (transliteration)
92.	意识到	**yìshídào**	to realize
93.	淑女	**shūnǚ**	fair maiden
94.	积极主动	**jījí zhǔdòng**	to actively take initiative
95.	策略	**cèlüè**	strategy
96.	被动	**bèidòng**	passive (i.e., to not take the initiative)
97.	命运	**mìngyùn**	fate

Discussion questions (discuss in English or Chinese):

1. In your personal life, do you have a favorite way of doing something that doesn't seem to work well for you anymore? If so, why haven't you made a change already?

2. We all know how foolish it is to "wait for more rabbits by a stump." So why are there so many people (even some very smart ones) who are keen on gambling because they hit the jackpot once before?

3. Can you think of any aspect in the governance of your country that reminds you of "waiting for more rabbits by a stump"? Choose any one aspect, and suggest a change in policy or law that would be in keeping with modern times.

When the City Gate Burns, Fish in the Moat Suffer Disaster

Once upon a time in ancient China, a fire broke out at a city gate next to the moat that protected the city from attack. One of the fish in the moat caught sight of the fire. Alarmed, he called out to his neighbor and the two of them had the following conversation:

RED FISH: This is going to be a huge calamity for the city's inhabitants! How will they escape?

BLUE FISH: Well, at least we're safe! There's no way the fire can reach us here in the water.

RED FISH: The fire is spreading fast, and everyone inside is trapped!

BLUE FISH: Look here, all of us are just little fish in the moat. We're lucky to escape being caught and cooked as gourmet meals. We can't worry about those people up there. What have they ever done for us anyway?

RED FISH: Oh look! They've called the fire brigade from the countryside, and everyone is coming with buckets to get water to put out the fire!

BLUE FISH: Yipes! They are scooping out all the water from the moat! Aghhhh! The water is almost gone! What will become of us?

RED FISH: Oh no, we are doomed!

This conversation ended quickly as the fish scrambled for cover in the lower depths of the moat. But it wasn't long before all the fish in the moat were flopping on the muddy bottom of an empty moat, gasping their last breaths.

城门失火，殃及池鱼

在古代的中国，有一天离护城河不远的一座城门着火了。护城河里的一条鱼最早发现了火灾，惊慌地告诉了邻居，于是两条鱼就有了下面的这段对话：

红鱼：这下子城里的百姓要遭殃了！他们往哪里逃呢？

蓝鱼：没事儿，至少咱们是安全的，火是不可能烧到咱们这里的。

红鱼：不得了啦，火越烧越大了，百姓都困在城里了！

蓝鱼：嗨，咱们只是这护城河里的小鱼。没人把咱们抓去做成美食吃了就够幸运的了。你瞎操什么心呢？再说了，他们又为咱们做过什么好事儿呢？

红鱼：快看呀，他们从外边叫了救火队来了，大家都带着桶，准备打水灭火呢！

蓝鱼：糟了！他们要把护城河里的水都舀光了！哎呀，水快没了！我们怎么办呐！

红鱼：天哪，我们完了！

两条鱼赶紧结束了对话，急忙游往护城河低处有水的地方。没过多久，护城河里的鱼都在淤泥里上下翻滚，在临死前张着大嘴拼命地呼气。

This fable is encapsulated in the proverb: "When the city wall burns, fish in the moat suffer disaster." This is a metaphor for the calamities that befall innocents in the lower ranks of society when an incident or conflict breaks out at a higher level. The fable is sad enough in itself, but the historical background of this proverb is an even darker story of betrayal, warfare and mass destruction.

Throughout Chinese history, times of dynastic change and periods of disunity were fraught with chaos and bloodshed. One of these was the Northern and Southern Dynasties period (386–589 CE). By 535, the country had split into three states—two in the north and one in the south—which alternated between open warfare and detente. All three were prone to internal upheavals, so that none could sustain its rule for more than a few decades.

Within this period of conflict and turmoil, the most stable and prosperous regime was that of Emperor Wu of Liang, whose rule lasted 47 years (502–549 CE). But even his empire was ultimately brought down by a scoundrel general by the name of Hou Jing, who originated from the Eastern Wei empire and who betrayed his own ruler by capitulating first to Western Wei, and then to Liang. Hou Jing's capitulation lured Emperor Wu into thinking that he could bring all of China under his rule through military conquest. After Liang was defeated in one of the early campaigns, Minister Du Bi of Eastern Wei issued a proclamation to Emperor Wu, in which he sternly warned the emperor that if he refuses to desist from further war, his country will be plunged into a bloodbath.

The proverb "when the city wall burns, fish in the moat suffer disaster" became the most memorable phrase used in that historical proclamation. Du Bi's proclamation did not focus on how the emperor and his officials would be captured and executed, but on the death and suffering of the ordinary people. With these words, Du Bi was appealing to Emperor Wu's conscience and reminding him of his moral responsibility to his people. Alas, the emperor was not persuaded. Sure enough, within a few months, Hou Jing mounted an insurrection which led to the destruction of the Liang empire and the death of the emperor.

这则寓言说的正是"城门失火，殃及池鱼"这一谚语，用来比喻上层的失误或者争斗给下层无辜的人民造成巨大的灾难。这则寓言本身已经够让人难过了，而它的历史背景是一个更黑暗的、充满背叛、战争以及人民遭殃的故事。

在中国历史上，改朝换代和国土分裂的年代里总是充满了战乱和血腥。南北朝(385–589)就是这样的一个时期。公元535年，整个国家分裂成了三个政权，两个在北方，一个在南方。这三个政权之间时而相互争战，时而维持和平。这三个政权各自也都充满了内部争斗，因而每个政权持续的时间也都不超过几十年。在这个动荡不安的时期，梁武帝的政权算是最稳定的，而他统治的国土也是最繁荣的。梁武帝在位47年 (502–549)，但最后被无恶不作的侯景将军所灭。侯景本来在东魏效力，但他后来两次叛乱，先投降到西魏，后又投降到梁朝。侯景归顺梁朝让梁武帝误以为自己可以利用军事力量统一全中国。梁武帝打了一次败仗以后，东魏的大臣杜弼向梁武帝递交了一篇檄文，严厉地告诫梁武帝，如果不停止战争，他的整个国家将卷入一场大屠杀。

"城门失火，殃及池鱼"成为了这篇檄梁文中最令人难忘的经典名句。杜弼在檄梁文里并没有强调皇帝和他的官员可能被俘虏和处决，而是把重点放在了无辜的平民百姓可能因战乱死去和遭受巨大的灾难。杜弼用"城门失火，殃及池鱼"的比喻，唤醒梁武帝的良心，提醒他对百姓应该承担的道德义务。可惜呀，皇帝并没有听从杜弼的劝告。果然，没过几个月，侯景再次叛乱，最终灭了梁朝，害死了梁武帝。

The good minister Du Bi went down in history as a hero, but within his lifetime and in his own country, he too fell victim to treachery. For his forthrightness and desire to stem corruption, he made political enemies who smeared him by accusing him of corruption. These false accusations resulted in his execution, although he was posthumously exonerated ten years later.

东魏的大臣杜弼在历史上是一位英雄，但是他活着的时候，也遭到奸臣的陷害。杜弼做官很清廉，常向皇帝直谏贪官污吏，因此在宫廷里有很多政敌，污蔑他收受贿赂。杜弼因为这一不实的指控被处决了，但十年之后得到了平反昭雪。

The Chinese Proverb

城	门	失	火，	殃	及	池	鱼
chéng	mén	shī	huǒ,	yāng	jí	chí	yú
walled city	gate	to have a mishap	fire	calamity	to reach	moat	fish

Literal meaning: When the city gate catches fire, disaster befalls the fish in the moat.

Connotation: When a conflict or incident occurs high up, innocent people below will suffer the most.

The original source: "Proclamation Issued to Liang on behalf of Eastern Wei," by Du Bi, Northern Qi Dynasty, 547 CE《为东魏檄梁文》，公元547年北齐杜弼著。

Vocabulary

1.	护城河	hùchénghé	moat (lit. "protect city river")
2.	着火	zháohuǒ	to catch on fire
3.	火灾	huǒzāi	fire disaster
4.	惊慌	jīnghuāng	alarmed
5.	邻居	línjū	neighbor
6.	遭殃	zāoyāng	to suffer disaster
7.	困	kùn	to be stranded
8.	抓	zhuā	to catch
9.	幸运	xìngyùn	to be fortunate
10.	瞎操心	xiā cāoxīn	to be worried over nothing
11.	救火队	jiùhuǒ duì	fire brigade
12.	桶	tǒng	bucket

13.	灭火	mièhuǒ	to extinguish a fire
14.	舀光	yǎoguāng	to bale out all the water
15.	赶紧	gǎnjǐn	to do something in a hurry
16.	淤泥	yūní	sludge, silt
17.	翻滚	fāngǔn	to flop around
18.	拼命	pīnmìng	with all one's might
19.	呼气	hūqì	to gasp
20.	谚语	yànyǔ	proverb, adage
21.	比喻	bǐyù	to make an analogy; a metaphor
22.	失误	shīwù	mistake, blunder
23.	争斗	zhēngdòu	to fight
24.	无辜	wúgū	innocent, blameless
25.	灾难	zāinàn	disaster
26.	充满	chōngmǎn	to be full of ...
27.	背叛	bèipàn	treachery
28.	改朝换代	gǎicháo huàndài	dynastic change
29.	分裂	fēnliè	to break up, to tear apart
30.	战乱	zhànluàn	war and chaos
31.	血腥	xuèxīng	bloody; bloodshed
32.	政权	zhèngquán	regime
33.	时而⋯ 时而⋯	shíér...shíér...	sometimes ..., sometimes ...
34.	争战	zhēngzhàn	to fight wars
35.	维持	wéichí	to maintain, to sustain
36.	内部	nèibù	internal
37.	争斗	zhēngdòu	struggles
38.	动荡不安	dòngdàng bù'ān	full of upheaval and unrest
39.	稳定	wěndìng	stable
40.	繁荣	fánróng	prosperous
41.	无恶不作	wú è búzuò	to stop at no evil (lit. "no evil not do")
42.	灭	miè	to destroy, to annihilate
43.	效力	xiàolì	to serve
44.	叛乱	pànluàn	to betray, to mount a rebellion; insurrection, rebellion
45.	投降	tóuxiáng	to surrender

46.	归顺	guīshùn	to submit allegiance to
47.	误以为	wù yǐwéi	to mistakenly think
48.	败仗	bàizhàng	a lost battle
49.	大臣	dàchén	high official
50.	递交	dìjiāo	to deliver (a document)
51.	檄文	xíwén	official denunciation of the enemy
52.	严厉	yánlì	stern
53.	告诫	gàojiè	to warn; a warning
54.	卷入	juǎnrù	to be embroiled in
55.	屠杀	túshā	massacre
56.	经典	jīngdiǎn	classic
57.	强调	qiángdiào	to stress, to emphasize
58.	俘虏	fúlǔ	to be captured (as a prisoner of war)
59.	处决	chǔjué	to execute; to be executed
60.	平民	píngmín	the common people
61.	遭受	zāoshòu	to suffer
62.	唤醒	huànxǐng	to rouse, to awaken
63.	良心	liángxīn	conscience
64.	承担	chéngdān	to bear (a responsibility)
65.	义务	yìwù	duty, responsibility
66.	听从	tīngcóng	to listen to and follow
67.	劝告	quàngào	persuasion
68.	奸臣	jiānchén	treacherous court official
69.	陷害	xiànhài	to trump up a charge against someone
70.	清廉	qīnglián	honest and upright
71.	直谏	zhíjiàn	to advice (the emperor) straightforwardly
72.	贪官污吏	tānguān wūlì	corrupt officials
73.	宫廷	gōngtíng	court
74.	政敌	zhèngdí	political enemy
75.	污蔑	wūmiè	to slander, to smear
76.	贿赂	huìlù	bribe
77.	不实	bùshí	untrue
78.	指控	zhǐkòng	accusation; to accuse
79.	平反昭雪	píngfǎn zhāoxuě	to be exonerated

The Collateral Damage of Divorce

Just as a fire at the city gate brings suffering to the fish in the moat, divorce often results in suffering for the children involved. This is why some unhappy couples wait until their children are grown and have left home before raising the issue of divorce. These parents deserve our respect for sacrificing their own happiness for the sake of their children. If they both truly love their children and exert their best efforts to raise them together, they still have a good chance of becoming good partners in the most challenging and rewarding endeavor of their lives. Over time, their cooperation may even put out the "fire at the city gate" so "the fish in the moat" will be spared.

Discussion questions (discuss in English or Chinese):

1. Have you ever encountered a situation where a conflict between two high-ranking rivals resulted in great collateral damage to the innocent people under them?

2. Can you apply the proverb in this chapter to a current event in the international arena?

3. In reference to trade wars, how do you think smaller countries are impacted by the decisions of the world's most powerful trading nations?

4. During China's dynastic change from the Ming to the Qing, the Manchus attacked Korea in order to gain its allegiance. This tragic episode in Korean history is portrayed in the novel *Namhansanseong*, and the subsequent film based on the novel. After looking up some information about this novel or film, comment on how it relates to the theme of this chapter.

离婚的代价

正如城门失火会殃及池塘里的鱼一样，一对夫妻离婚也常给孩子造成伤害。因此，一些婚姻并不幸福的夫妻会等到孩子长大离开家以后才提出离婚。这些为了孩子而牺牲自己幸福的夫妇令人敬佩。如果他们真的很爱孩子，并且尽最大的努力共同把孩子抚养成人，那么在养育孩子这件最为艰巨，同时又是最令人有成就感的任务中，他们很有可能成为很好的合作伙伴。久而久之，夫妇之间的合作甚至有可能扑灭"城门上的火灾"，而"池塘里的鱼"也可能得以幸免。

Vocabulary

80.	代价	dàijià	price, cost (often metaphorical)
81.	正如	zhèngrú	just as
82.	夫妻	fūqī	husband and wife
83.	伤害	shānghài	damage, harm
84.	幸福	xìngfú	happy
85.	牺牲	xīshēng	to sacrifice
86.	敬佩	jìngpèi	to esteem
87.	抚养	fǔyǎng	to raise (children)
88.	养育	yǎngyù	to bring up, to rear (children)
89.	艰巨	jiānjù	arduous
90.	成就感	chéngjiù-gǎn	sense of accomplishment
91.	合作伙伴	hézuò huǒbàn	partner in cooperation
92.	久而久之	jiǔ ér jiǔ zhī	in the course of time, as time passes
93.	扑灭	pūmiè	to extinguish (a fire), to wipe out
94.	幸免	xìngmiǎn	to spare (someone); to be spared from ...

The Old Frontiersman
Who Lost His Horse

The Han dynasty was arguably the greatest dynasty in Chinese history. It was China's second dynasty, but its predecessor the Qin dynasty lasted only fourteen years, whereas the Han dynasty spanned more than four centuries (206 BCE–202 CE)—longer than any other dynasty in Chinese history. To this day, the Chinese refer to themselves as the "Han people" and the official name for standard Chinese is the "Han language."

The first half of the Han dynasty saw great territorial expansion toward the south and the northwest. It was during this period that China's territory was extended all the way to the Tarim Basin in Central Asia and the Silk Road to the West was established. The nomadic peoples to the North and Northwest, collectively called "Xiongnu" by the Chinese, were formidable foes. China's borderlands were constantly fought over in major battles as well as minor skirmishes. The story in this chapter gives us a glimpse of how large-scale historical events impacted the ordinary people living along China's frontier.

In one of the frontier settlements in the early Han dynasty, an old man lived with his son. Having lost his wife early on, the old man was especially grateful to have a son to support him in his old age.

The old man had an uncanny knack for fortune telling, so he was not too worried about his own future. One day, the family's horse disappeared and everyone presumed that it had crossed the border into Xiongnu territory. Knowing that it would be difficult to retrieve the horse, all the villagers came to console the old man. To their surprise, he replied nonchalantly, "How do we know this is not a blessing in disguise?" Lo and behold, a few weeks later, the old man's horse came home, bringing with it a sprightly mare from the land of the Xiongnu. Now everyone realized that the horse had gone abroad and found itself a mate! All the villagers congratulated the man for having acquired another horse. But again the old man surprised them with his reply, saying "How do we

塞翁失马，焉知非福

在中国历史上，最伟大的朝代无疑是汉朝。汉朝是中国历史上第二个皇朝，但前面的秦朝只统治了14年，而汉朝却延续了四百多年（公元前206年–公元202年），超过了中国历史上的任何一个朝代。到今天，占人口绝大多数的民族是"汉人"，而标准中文的正式名称是"汉语"。

汉朝的疆域在其前半期向南边和西北边大大地扩展了，而正是在这个时期，中国的领土一直延伸到了中亚的塔里木盆地，而丝绸之路也是在这个时候开通的。汉人把生活在塞北和塞外西北边的游牧民族统称为匈奴。对汉人来说，匈奴是很强悍的敌人。在塞外边境一带，大大小小的战事常年不断。下面的这个故事就让我们看到那段历史对生活在塞外的普通百姓有什么影响。

汉朝初年，一位老人和儿子住在塞外的一个村子里。老人的妻子很早就过世了，所以他感觉自己晚年有儿子照顾是很幸运的。老人会算卦，因此对自己的未来不太担心。有一天，家里的马不见了，村民们都猜测那匹马一定是跑到匈奴的地界去了。大家都知道这样的情况下，马很难找回来，所以村民们都安慰老人。没想到老人淡然地说："你们怎么知道这不是一件好事呢？"过了几个星期，老人的马居然回来了，而且还从匈奴地界上带回来一匹神采奕奕的母马。村里的人听说老人的马到国外去溜了一圈，还给自己带回来一个新娘，就都来恭贺老人。然而老人的回答又一次让大家很

know this is not a tragedy in the making?" At that moment, everything seemed fine. The family was well-off and they had two fine horses that might even bless them with foals in the near future. But a few days later, disaster struck. The man's son loved to ride horses, but the mare from the land of the Xiongnu was not used to being mounted by a foreign rider. When the son mounted the mare for the first time, she reared up and threw him to the ground. The young man heard his left leg snap and instantly felt a shooting pain. In an instant, he was crippled for life. Once again, the villagers consoled the old man. This time they were not surprised when he said in reply, "How do we know this is not a blessing in disguise?"

吃惊:"我们怎么知道这不是一件坏事呢?"当时,家里的一切看上去都挺好的:日子过得不错,家里有两匹马,说不定很快还会给家里添小马驹呢。谁也没想到,没过几天家里就大祸临头了。儿子很喜欢骑马,可是那匹来自匈奴的母马不习惯让一个外国人骑在背上。儿子第一次骑母马的时候,母马一跃而起,把小伙子重重地摔在地上。小伙子听到他的左腿咔嚓一声,随后感觉到一阵剧痛。就那么一下子,小伙子的腿骨折了。在余下的人生里,他将成为一个残疾人。村民们又来安慰老人,而老人也照例回答"谁知道这不是一件好事呢?"不过这一次大家对老人这样的回答已经不再感到惊讶了。

A year later the Xiongnu launched a major attack against the Chinese. The Han emperor immediately recruited all able-bodied men in the frontier villages to combat them. Of those who were sent into battle, nine out of ten perished. However the crippled young man was spared and the old man still had his son to support him in his old age.

The author ends his story with this conclusion: "Good fortune can turn to disaster, and disaster can turn to good fortune. The swing of the pendulum from one extreme to the other is endless; its mystery is beyond our ability to fathom." To this day, a person who knows the frontiersman's wisdom may console himself and find a silver lining in any misfortune that may befall him.

The Chinese Proverb

塞	翁	失	马,	焉	知	非	福
sài	wēng	shī	mǎ,	yān	zhī	fēi	fú
border pass	old man	to lose	horse,	how	to know	not	blessing

Literal meaning: The old man at the frontier pass lost his horse; how do we know it's not a blessing (in disguise)?

Connotation: An apparent misfortune can sometimes be a blessing in disguise and what appears to be good fortune may turn out to be a disaster. We humans cannot see into the future to predict what will happen. Therefore, we should accept losses and gains with equanimity and not get too excited over them one way or the other.

The original source: "Lessons from the World of Man," a chapter from the book *Huainanzi* (*Master of Huainan*), by Liu An (179–122 BCE), Prince of Huainan, and his entourage, of the Western Han dynasty. 《淮南子·人间训》, 西汉淮南王刘安(公元前179–122年)及其门客著。

一年后，匈奴大举进犯中原，汉朝皇帝随即在塞外的村庄招募所有壮丁上战场抵御匈奴。那些上战场的人，十有八九阵亡了。那位摔断了腿的年轻人因为上不了战场而保住了性命，而老人也因此很幸运，在晚年还有儿子在身边照顾。

在故事的最后作者得出了这样的结语："好事可能变成坏事，坏事也可能变成好事。两者之间在不断地转化中，也是深不可测的。"今天，熟悉塞翁失马故事的人，不管遇到什么灾难，都可以用老人的智慧来安慰自己，并在不幸中看到光明的那一面。

Vocabulary

1.	无疑	**wúyí**	without a doubt
2.	皇朝	**huángcháo**	empire
3.	统治	**tǒngzhì**	to govern
4.	延续	**yánxù**	to continue; to carry on
5.	占	**zhàn**	to occupy
6.	绝大多数	**jué dà duōshù**	a great majority
7.	正式	**zhèngshì**	official, formal
8.	名称	**míngchēng**	name, designation
9.	疆域	**jiāngyù**	territory, domain
10.	扩展	**kuòzhǎn**	to expand
11.	领土	**lǐngtǔ**	territory
12.	延伸	**yánshēn**	to extend
13.	塔里木盆地	**Tǎlǐmù Péndì**	Tarim Basin
14.	丝绸之路	**sīchóu zhī lù**	Silk Road
15.	塞北和塞外	**sàiběi hé sàiwài**	region north of, and outside of the Great Wall

16.	统称	**tǒngchēng**	collectively called, generally known as
17.	匈奴	**Xiōngnú**	Huns
18.	强悍	**qiánghàn**	intrepid, formidable
19.	边境	**biānjìng**	border region
20.	常年	**chángnián**	year in, year out
21.	过世	**guòshì**	to pass away
22.	晚年	**wǎnnián**	in old age
23.	幸运	**xìngyùn**	fortunate
24.	算卦	**suànguà**	to tell fortune
25.	猜测	**cāicè**	to guess
26.	地界	**dìjiè**	territorial boundary
27.	安慰	**ānwèi**	to console
28.	淡然	**dànrán**	indifferent, cool, nonchalant
29.	居然	**jūrán**	to one's surprise, contrary to expectations
30.	神采奕奕	**shéncǎi yìyì**	high-spirited, beaming with vim and vigor
31.	溜一圈	**liū yìquān**	to take a stroll
32.	新娘	**xīnniáng**	bride
33.	恭贺	**gōnghè**	to congratulate
34.	吃惊	**chījīng**	to be startled
35.	添	**tiān**	to add, to increase
36.	马驹	**mǎjū**	foal
37.	大祸临头	**dàhuò líntóu**	a disaster befalls one
38.	一跃而起	**yí yuè ér qǐ**	to rise in one leap, to spring up suddenly
39.	摔	**shuāi**	to fall; to throw off
40.	咔嚓	**kāchā**	sound of something snapping

41.	剧痛	**jùtòng**	sharp pain
42.	骨折	**gǔzhé**	bone fracture
43.	余下	**yúxià**	remaining, rest of ...
44.	残疾人	**cánjírén**	handicapped person, a cripple
45.	照例	**zhàolì**	as usual
46.	惊讶	**jīngyà**	surprised
47.	大举	**dàjǔ**	to start up (something big)
48.	进犯	**jìnfàn**	invade
49.	中原	**zhōngyuán**	Central Plain (of China)
50.	随即	**suíjí**	following immediately, soon thereafter
51.	招募	**zhāomù**	to recruit (troops)
52.	壮丁	**zhuàngdīng**	able-bodied men
53.	战场	**zhànchǎng**	battlefield
54.	抵御	**dǐyù**	to resist, to withstand
55.	十有八九	**shí yǒu bājiǔ**	eight or nine out of ten
56.	阵亡	**zhènwáng**	to die in battle
57.	性命	**xìngmìng**	life
58.	结语	**jiéyǔ**	concluding remarks
59.	转化	**zhuǎnhuà**	to transform
60.	深不可测	**shēn bùkěcè**	so deep that it cannot be fathomed
61.	熟悉	**shúxī**	to be familiar with
62.	灾难	**zāinàn**	disaster
63.	智慧	**zhìhuì**	wisdom

Missing an Ill-fated Flight

For the Chinese, World War II was an eight-year-long conflict with Japan. Within that period some 14 million Chinese died and up to 100 million became refugees. My family was fortunate to have come through the war intact but another potential disaster was lurking around the corner.

The post-war period was a chaotic time. People relied on their personal connections to find jobs and to obtain goods and services. My father was employed as an English secretary to the director of CNRRA (Chinese National Relief and Rehabilitation Administration), the Chinese arm of UNRRA (the United Nations Relief and Rehabilitation Administration). At that time, all Chinese government agencies were being relocated from the wartime capital of Chongqing back to Nanjing. CNRRA was a well-funded agency, so the director, my father's boss, had the use of a government plane to shuttle himself back and forth between his duties in Chongqing and Nanjing. It was his prerogative to take a few extra people on each trip and he offered to take the wife and children of his secretary (my father) on one of the flights. But on the morning of our scheduled flight, he announced that he had arranged passage for us on a boat instead, as some other friends needed to go to Nanjing more urgently. My parents were of course disappointed, but they expressed appreciation for his thoughtfulness.

Just a couple of days later, even before we arrived in Nanjing, we heard the news that the plane that took off without us had disappeared. It was never found and all the passengers were presumed to have perished. We had only narrowly escaped their fate. Just like the old frontiersman who lost his horse, our family's loss turned out to be a blessing in disguise!

幸好没搭上那趟便机

对中国人来说，第二次世界大战就是八年的抗日战争。在那段时间里，大约1400万中国人丧生，近一亿人成为了难民。我本人的家庭还算幸运，全家人都平安地熬过了战争，不过在战后也险些遭遇了一场意想不到的灾难。

当时的情形很混乱，人们都得依靠个人的关系来找工作，来取得生活必需品和各种服务。我父亲受聘于中国善后救济总署，担任这个机构的英文秘书。那个时候，中国所有的政府机构都正在从战时的首都重庆迁回南京。中国善后救济总署是联合国善后救济总署的分支机构，是个经费充足的政府部门。因此总署的主任，即我父亲的老板，在他因公往返重庆和南京的时候，有政府的专机接送。而且主任每次出行，都有特权带几个人跟他一起搭乘飞机，所以他告诉秘书（我的父亲）下次可以带上妻子和孩子一起回南京。就在我们定好出行的那天早上，主任告知我们，因为另有一些人要急着回南京，所以他安排了我们乘船回去。我父母当然有点失望，不过他们还是感谢主任考虑得很周到。

没过两天，我们还没到南京的时候，就听说我们原本要搭乘的那架飞机失踪了。后来那架飞机一直没找到，机上的所有乘客想必都遇难了。就像塞翁失马一样，我们一家也因为没搭上那架飞机而保全了性命。

Vocabulary

64.	幸好	xìnghǎo	fortunately
65.	搭…便机	dā...biànjī	to hitch a plane ride (with someone)
66.	抗日战争	kàng Rì zhànzhēng	War of Resistance against Japan
67.	大约	dàyuē	approximately
68.	丧生	sàngshēng	to lose their lives
69.	难民	nànmín	refugees
70.	还算	háisuàn	can be counted as ...
71.	熬过	áoguò	to have endured through some hardship
72.	险些	xiǎnxiē	narrowly escaping (some misfortune), nearly
73.	遭遇	zāoyù	to encounter (misfortune)
74.	混乱	hùnluàn	chaotic
75.	依靠	yīkào	to rely on
76.	取得	qǔdé	to obtain, to attain
77.	品	pǐn	products, goods
78.	受聘于	shòupìnyú	to be employed by
79.	中国善后救济总署	Zhōngguó Shàn-hòu Jiùjì Zǒngshǔ	Chinese National Relief and Rehabilitation Administration (CNRRA)
80.	担任	dānrèn	to serve in the position of ...
81.	机构	jīgòu	organization
82.	秘书	mìshū	secretary
83.	迁回	qiānhuí	to move back to
84.	联合国善后救济总署	Liánhéguó Shàn-hòu Jiùjì Zǒngshǔ	United Nations Relief and Rehabilitation Administration (UNRRA)
85.	分支	fēnzhī	branch
86.	充足	chōngzú	sufficient, ample
87.	部门	bùmén	department
88.	主任	zhǔrèn	chairman, director
89.	即	jí	that is, i.e.
90.	老板	lǎobǎn	boss

91. 因公	yīngōng	due to official duty, on business
92. 往返	wǎngfǎn	going back and forth; round-trip
93. 专机	zhuānjī	chartered plane
94. 出行	chūxíng	to go on a journey
95. 特权	tèquán	special privilege
96. 搭乘	dāchéng	to travel on a certain conveyance (plane, boat, etc.)
97. 失望	shīwàng	to be disappointed
98. 考虑	kǎolǜ	to consider
99. 周到	zhōudào	thorough, thoughtful, attentive, considerate
100. 失踪	shīzōng	to disappear
101. 乘客	chéngkè	passengers
102. 遇难	yùnàn	to perish (in an accident)
103. 保全	bǎoquán	to preserve, to keep safe

Discussion questions (discuss in English or Chinese):

1. Have you ever failed to get something that you were sure you could get, like a date with someone, a certain job, or admission to a certain school, and then ended up with something even better? Can you tell about such an experience?

2. Everyone has had at least one experience where a misfortune turned out to be a blessing in disguise. While the converse is less frequent, it can happen. That is, a lucky break could turn out to be a disaster in the making. Can you tell about one or two such experiences that have happened to you or someone close to you?

3. What are some ways in which people in modern society mitigate the ups and downs of fortune? What about olden times? Are there differences in different cultures?

Pure Water Has No Fish; Scrupulous People Have No Friends

The proverb in the title of this chapter has appeared in numerous Chinese historical and literary works and it continues to be relevant today. In the following narrative, it is used in the context of China's first territorial expansion into Central Asia during the Han dynasty. A central figure in this expansion was Ban Chao (32–102 CE), and who came from a family of high officials in the Han court and was himself a military general, diplomat and explorer. He is credited with subduing the tribal peoples in the Tarim Basin and bringing them under Chinese rule during the second half of the first century. He accomplished all this through a combination of military conquests and diplomacy. All told, he served in this vast region for over three decades—the last eleven years in the capacity of Protector General (i.e., governor) of the region. His success helped open and secure the trade routes—later dubbed the "Silk Road"—to the West.

The biography of Ban Chao in the official Han dynastic history begins with these words: "He was a man of great ambition, but did not fret over details." This characterization of Ban Chao turned out to be the key to his success in governing the Western Regions.

In 102 CE when Ban Chao was already 70 and no longer in good health, the emperor granted his request to transfer back to the capital, and he passed away just a month after returning to Luoyang. But before he died, his successor Ren Shang, while preparing to embark for his new post, sought Ban Chao's advice based on his extensive experience. Ban Chao, not given to eloquent speeches, said the following: "I'm old and a bit befuddled now, but if you really want to hear my thoughts on governing the region, I'll offer you my humble opinion. Those who were sent to work on the frontier were never paragons of virtue to begin with.

水至清则无鱼，
人至察则无徒

在许多中国历史文学作品中，我们都曾看到过这个标题上的谚语。一直到现在，这个谚语还是很实用。下面这篇短文描述了中国在汉朝第一次向中亚扩张的情形，其中就使用了这个谚语。中国历史在这个时期的一个重要人物名叫班超（公元32–102）。班超来自一个高官家族，他本人是一位将军，也是一位外交家和探险家。在中国历史上，班超最著名的功绩是征服了在塔里木盆地的匈奴，并在第一世纪的后半期将西域的各部落纳入了汉王朝的统治之下。这些成就都是班超通过军事征服与外交策略相结合的办法取得的。总之，班超在西域这片辽阔的土地上运筹帷幄并征战了三十多年，而最后的十一年担任了西域的都护。在班超的治理下，西域开通并保障了通往西方的贸易通道，也就是后来人们所说的"丝绸之路"。

《后汉书·班超传》的开场白把班超的性格归纳得十分精确："他很有志向，但不拘小节。"班超的这一特征正是他能够成功治理西域的关键。

公元102年，班超年满70岁了，健康状况也不佳，就请求朝廷将他召回了京城洛阳，一个月以后就去世了。班超治理西域有很丰富的经验，因此在他去世之前，将要前往西域继任的任尚就来向他求教。班超并没有长篇大论地指教任尚，而只是告诉他："我年纪大了，也有点糊涂了。如果您真想听听我的建议的话，那照本人的拙见，塞外的那些吏士

In fact, they were all banished to those outposts for crimes. And then consider the Central Asian tribes—most of whom are uncivilized barbarians, difficult to discipline and easily corrupted. Now you are highly scrupulous and eager to get things done quickly. You should know that 'pure water has no fish and scrupulous people have no friends.' If you are too conscientious in your administration, you'll lose the cooperation of those below you. It is best to keep things simple and overlook minor infractions. Go easy on the people there; as long as the big picture is okay, that's good enough."

Ren Shang apparently had no use for Ban Chao's advice, for he privately said to a close friend, "I thought Ban Chao was going to give me some clever strategies, but I received nothing but platitudes from him." Sure enough, within a few years after Ren Shang took office, the turmoil that Ban Chao had warned him of began to unfold. The tribes in the Western Regions began to rebel and Ren Shang was recalled to the capital to answer to the emperor.

本来就不是贤德之人，大多是因为犯了罪才被派到边远的地域去的。而中亚的那些部落也大多是不开化的蛮夷，很难安抚，也很容易挑起事端。您本人审慎正直，做事急于求成。但您应该知道'水至清则无鱼，人至察则无徒'。如果您政务太严苛了，下属就很难依附您。处理政务最好简单一些，不计较下属的小过错，以宽厚的胸怀包容那里的人。只要大事抓好了，就已经够好的了。"班超的话，任尚显然没听进去，因为他私下告诉一个亲信："我以为班超会告诉我一些治理西域的金科玉律，其实我从他那儿什么好的建议都没得到。"不出所料，任尚接管西域几年之内，班超曾经警告过他的动乱就出现了，西域的部落相继叛乱，而任尚也被召回京城向皇上禀报去了。

The Chinese proverb

水	至	清	则	无		鱼
shuǐ	zhì	qīng	zé	wú		yú
water	extremely	clear	then	to have no		fish

人	至	察	则	无		徒
rén	zhì	chá	zé	wú		tú
person	extremely	scrupulous	then	to have no		friends, followers

Literal meaning: No fish are found in extremely clear waters; an extremely scrupulous person has no friends (or followers)

Connotation: It is difficult for people to befriend or follow someone who is too perfect. In the professional world, people do not like to work with or under overly strict people. Therefore, it is best to cut one's friends and colleagues some slack.

The original source: "Biography of Ban Chao," in *History of the Latter Han Dynasty*, by Fan Ye of the Southern Dynasty of Song, ca. 450 CE. 《后汉书•班超传》。南朝宋•范晔编撰（约公元450年）

Vocabulary

1.	标题	**biāotí**	title
2.	谚语	**yànyǔ**	proverb, common saying
3.	描述	**miáoshù**	to depict
4.	扩张	**kuòzhāng**	to expand
5.	人物	**rénwù**	personage, important figure
6.	家族	**jiāzú**	clan, family (extended)
7.	将军	**jiāngjun**	military general
8.	外交家	**wàijiāojiā**	diplomat
9.	探险家	**tànxiǎnjiā**	explorer
10.	功绩	**gōngjì**	merit and achievements
11.	征服	**zhēngfú**	to conquer
12.	塔里木盆地	**Tǎlǐmù Péndì**	Tarim Basin
13.	匈奴	**Xiōngnú**	Huns

14. 西域	**Xīyù**	Western Region
15. 部落	**bùluò**	tribes
16. 纳入	**nàrù**	to incorporate into
17. 统治	**tǒngzhì**	to rule over
18. 成就	**chéngjiù**	accomplishments
19. 策略	**cèlüè**	strategy
20. 辽阔	**liáokuò**	vast
21. 运筹帷幄	**yùnchóu wéiwò**	to devise campaign strategy (lit. "to make plans in an army tent")
22. 征战	**zhēngzhàn**	to go on military expeditions
23. 担任	**dānrèn**	to serve in the capacity of ...
24. 都护	**dūhù**	Protector General, governor
25. 保障	**bǎozhàng**	to secure; security
26. 贸易	**màoyì**	trade
27. 丝绸之路	**sīchóu zhī lù**	Silk Road
28. 后汉书·班超传	**Hòu Hàn Shū· Bān Chāo Zhuàn**	*History of the Latter Han Dynasty, Biography of Ban Chao*
29. 开场白	**kāichǎngbái**	opening statement
30. 性格	**xìnggé**	character, personality
31. 归纳	**guīnà**	to sum up
32. 精确	**jīngquè**	precise
33. 志向	**zhìxiàng**	ambition
34. 不拘小节	**bùjū xiǎojié**	not concerned about trifles
35. 关键	**guānjiàn**	crucial; key point
36. 佳	**jiā**	(formal) good, fine
37. 朝廷	**cháotíng**	imperial court
38. 召回	**zhàohuí**	to call back
39. 继任	**jìrèn**	to succeed (someone) in a position
40. 求教	**qiújiào**	to seek instruction
41. 长篇大论	**chángpiān dàlùn**	to speak at length, to be verbose
42. 指教	**zhǐjiào**	to give advice

43. 糊涂	**hútu**	muddle-headed
44. 拙见	**zhuōjiàn**	humble opinion
45. 塞外	**Sàiwài**	region beyond the Great Wall
46. 吏士	**lìshì**	officers and clerks
47. 贤德	**xiándé**	virtuous
48. 犯罪	**fànzuì**	to commit a crime
49. 开化	**kāihuà**	civilized
50. 蛮夷	**mányí**	"barbarians" (non-Han ethnic groups)
51. 安抚	**ānfǔ**	to placate
52. 挑起事端	**tiǎoqǐ shìduān**	to raise disturbance
53. 审慎	**shěnshèn**	cautious, circumspect
54. 急于求成	**jíyú qiúchéng**	anxious to get things done
55. 政务	**zhèngwù**	governance
56. 严苛	**yánkē**	strict and harsh
57. 下属	**xiàshǔ**	underlings
58. 依附	**yīfù**	to submit to (a leader)
59. 处理	**chǔlǐ**	to manage

60.	计较	jìjiào	to fret about small matters
61.	过错	guòcuò	faults, mistakes
62.	宽厚	kuānhòu	magnanimous
63.	胸怀	xiōnghuái	heart, mind
64.	包容	bāoróng	lenient, broadminded
65.	抓	zhuā	to grasp, to take charge of (colloquial)
66.	显然	xiǎnrán	obviously, apparently
67.	私下	sīxià	privately
68.	亲信	qīnxìn	trusted follower
69.	金科玉律	jīnkē yùlǜ	golden rule
70.	不出所料	bùchū suǒ liào	as expected (lit. "did not exceed what was expected")
71.	警告	jǐnggào	warning
72.	动乱	dòngluàn	uprising
73.	相继	xiāngjì	one after another
74.	叛乱	pànluàn	rebellion
75.	禀报	bǐngbào	to report (to a superior)

Learning to be a Friend of "Perfect" People

Helen has become my lifelong friend, but it took me a while and a bit of soul-searching to reach this point in my relationship with her. We started out as colleagues in the same field. Although I thought of her as a peer, she was more professional and meticulous than I in every way. I admired her and saw her as a role model. I also wanted very much to be her friend but I had a hard time feeling warm toward her. I also noticed that Helen did not have other close friends either. This puzzled me, so I tried to think what was wrong with Helen that made it hard for me to approach her. Helen had extremely high standards for her staff, and even higher standards for herself. She had great leadership ability, and gave constructive criticism to others. Then it dawned on me that she was too perfect! So what's wrong with being too perfect? Nothing! Then it occurred to me that maybe the problem was with me!

Eventually, I realized that how I felt about Helen was a result of Helen's influence on my own self-image. And yes, I felt inadequate when I compared myself to her. So I consciously tried to focus on all the wonderful things about myself when I was with Helen, and to imagine that Helen appreciated those qualities in me as well. This revelation taught me how to become friends with Helen as well as many other people I admired. A corollary lesson that I learned was this: If I want to have friends, I must not seem too "perfect," and I should deliberately display my foibles, with good humor of course. In truth, no one is perfect!

Once I saw Helen as a lovable friend, I realized that she was not perfect after all. She could lighten up and learn to have a little more sense of humor like me! Now with the help of the proverb "pure water has no fish; scrupulous people have no friends," I will never forget the lesson learned from my friendship with Helen.

完美无缺的朋友

我和终生的朋友海伦之间的友情来之不易，是经过一番深度自省才建立起来的。我们因为是同行而相互认识的。尽管我们俩是同龄人，不过我眼中的海伦在各方面都比我专业，也更加一丝不苟。我很佩服她，把她看作我的人生楷模，也很想跟她交朋友。不过我发现自己心里感觉不到对海伦的亲切感。我也注意到海伦并没有其他亲密的朋友。这让我有点迷惑：海伦到底有什么问题，让我很难亲近她呢？海伦对下属的要求极高，对自己更是严苛。她有很强的领导能力，也很善于给别人提出建设性的意见。想着想着，我就意识到海伦的问题是她太完美了！太完美有什么不对吗？当然没有！想到这里，我又感觉到问题可能是出在我自己身上！

最终，我才意识到我对海伦缺乏亲切感是因为她影响了我的自我形象。可不是嘛，我在海伦身边就感觉自己不够好。后来我跟海伦在一起的时候，就刻意地去关注自己所有的优点，想着海伦也应该会欣赏我的这些优点。这样一来，我就知道怎么跟海伦交朋友了，也知道怎么跟所有我佩服的人交朋友了。由此类推出来的道理就是：如果我要别人亲近我的话，就不能显得太完美，而应该有意地显现出自己一些无关紧要的小缺点。说实在的，世上没有完美的人。

一旦我发现海伦是个很可爱的朋友以后，就觉得她其实也并没有那么完美。她应该放松一点儿，也可以向我学习学习，多一点儿幽默感！"水至清则无鱼，人至察则无徒"这个谚语很好地概括了我与海伦交朋友的心得，使我终生难忘。

Vocabulary

76.	完美无缺	**wánměi wúquē**	perfect and flawless
77.	终生	**zhōngshēng**	lifelong
78.	来之不易	**lái zhī búyì**	to attain through some difficulty; hard to come by
79.	自省	**zìxǐng**	self-examination, soul-searching
80.	同行	**tóngháng**	in the same profession
81.	相互	**xiānghù**	mutually
82.	同龄	**tónglíng**	of the same age
83.	专业	**zhuānyè**	professional
84.	一丝不苟	**yìsī bùgǒu**	extremely conscientious and meticulous
85.	佩服	**pèifu**	to admire, to esteem
86.	楷模	**kǎimó**	role model
87.	亲切感	**qīnqiègǎn**	warm feelings
88.	亲密	**qīnmì**	intimate
89.	迷惑	**míhuò**	puzzled, perplexed
90.	亲近	**qīnjìn**	to be close to (someone)
91.	善于	**shànyú**	to be skilled at …
92.	建设性	**jiànshèxìng**	constructive
93.	意识到	**yìshi dào**	to realize
94.	缺乏	**quēfá**	to lack
95.	自我形象	**zìwǒ xíngxiàng**	self-image
96.	刻意	**kèyì**	deliberately
97.	关注	**guānzhù**	to pay attention to
98.	优点	**yōudiǎn**	strong points
99.	欣赏	**xīnshǎng**	to appreciate
100.	类推	**lèituī**	to reason by analogy
101.	道理	**dàolǐ**	principle, truth
102.	显得	**xiǎnde**	to appear

103. 显现出	xiǎnxiànchū	to reveal
104. 无关紧要	wúguān jǐnyào	inconsequential, unimportant
105. 缺点	quēdiǎn	shortcomings
106. 一旦	yídàn	once, as soon as
107. 放松	fàngsōng	to relax
108. 幽默感	yōumògǎn	sense of humor
109. 概括	gàikuò	to summarize, to put it simply
110. 心得	xīndé	what one learned from an experience

Discussion questions (discuss in English or Chinese):

1. Do you personally know of anyone who is "too perfect" to have friends? Do you think that someone might be lonely? If you feel empathy for that someone, would you try to help?

2. In our contemporary world, do teachers have anything to learn from the proverb in this chapter?

3. The British colonization of Australia began in 1788, with the setting up of penal colonies. Do you think there may be similarities between how Ban Chao governed the Western Regions and how the British governed their Australian colonies?

Bo Le Recognizes a Superb Horse

According to legend, there was an immortal in heaven by the name of Bo Le who looked after horses. Here on earth during the Spring and Autumn period there was a man by the name of Sun Yang who loved horses and knew them like his own kin, so people started calling him Bo Le. This living Bo Le was commissioned by the King of Chu to purchase the finest horse that could be found—one that could run 1000 *li* in a day.* Bo Le promised to do his best, but he made it clear to the King that he must be patient, for there weren't many horses that could run 1000 *li* in a day, and he would need time to search for one far and wide. Bo Le traveled to many kingdoms, including Yan and Zhao, which were known for their fine horses. Still he didn't find a horse that met his high standards.

Then one day as he was returning home, Bo Le saw a horse pulling a wagon laden with salt trudging laboriously up a steep slope. The horse was so exhausted that it was panting with each step. Bo Le always had a soft spot for horses so he instinctively walked right up to the horse. As soon as the horse saw Bo Le approaching, its eyes opened wide and it raised its head and neighed loudly as though pouring its heart out to Bo Le. From the sound of the horse's voice, Bo Le knew immediately that he had stumbled upon an extraordinary steed. He said to the wagoneer, "This horse can outrun any other horse on the battlefield, but it is not as good as an ordinary horse for the job of pulling a wagon. Why don't you let me buy it from you?"

The wagoneer never thought his horse was anything special. It didn't have much strength for pulling a wagon, and even though it ate a lot, it was as skinny as a bag of bones. This man who is offering to pay good money for this horse must be a fool, he thought. But hey, it's a good deal for me! So without hesitation, he accepted Bo Le's offer.

---

* The term "1000 *li*" is a figurative way of expressing a high number. Technically, 1 *li* = ½ km, or approximately ⅓ mile. So 1000 *li*, if taken literally, would be over 300 miles.

伯乐相马

传说中，天国里管理马匹的神仙名叫伯乐。在人间，春秋时期有一个叫孙阳的人对马就像自己的亲人一样了解，所以大家都叫他伯乐。楚王命伯乐遍寻天下，买来日行千里的骏马。[*] 伯乐领命，但告诉楚王得耐心等待，因为千里马并不多见，他得到处走走看看，慢慢寻找。伯乐走了很多国家，包括盛产良马的燕国和赵国，但是都没找到他理想中的千里马。

　　有一天，伯乐在回家的路上看见一匹马拉着装满盐的车子，在陡坡上吃力地前行。那匹马看上去已经筋疲力尽了，每走一步都气喘吁吁。伯乐一向跟马很亲近，很自然地就走到马旁边。那匹马一看见伯乐走过来，便睁大了眼睛，仰天长啸，好像要对伯乐倾诉什么。伯乐立刻从马嘶声中断定这是一匹难得的骏马，于是就对赶车人说："这匹马如果驰骋在疆场上，任何马都不如它，可是用它来拉车，还不如一匹普通的马。你把它卖给我吧？"赶车人从来都没觉得这匹马很特别，吃得多，却拉不动车，而且看上去骨瘦如柴。赶车人心想这个人愿意出高价买它，一定是个大傻瓜，不过对自己来说还是很合算啊！这样想着，他就毫不犹豫地接受了伯乐的提议。

---

* 这里的"千里"是一种比喻。实际上，1里等于半公里，也就是大约1/3英里。因此，确切地说1千里就是300多英里。

Having accomplished his mission, Bo Le went straight back to the State of Chu with his prize horse. As he led the horse into the palace, he patted its neck and said, "I have found you a good master!" In response the horse went clippity-clop with its hooves on the pavement, stretched its neck toward the clouds above and let out a thunderous neigh. Hearing the neighing of the horse, the King came out to see what the commotion was all about. Pointing to the horse Bo Le said to the King, "Your highness, I've brought you the finest 1000-*li* horse. Take a look!"

What the King saw was just a skinny horse, nothing but a bag of bones. In fact he felt Bo Le was mocking him, so he angrily snapped, "I asked you to go buy me a horse because I thought you knew how to appraise horses. What kind of a horse is this?! It has a hard time just walking, how can it run on the battlefield?" Bo Le kept his cool as he explained to the King, "Your highness, in all honesty, what you see here is truly a 1000-*li* horse. It's just that it's been misused for pulling wagons all its life and has not been properly nourished, so it looks very skinny. With proper nourishment and care, in half a month it will become the horse it was meant to be. With all due respect to your majesty, why would I tell you anything but the truth?" The great King was not entirely convinced but he was touched by Bo Le's sincerity, so he decided to give the horse a chance to prove itself. He ordered his personal groom to take the skinny horse under his care, provide it with the best possible diet and let it rest as much as it desired. For the first time in its life, the horse was in horse heaven! Sure enough, this skinny creature soon turned into a most able-bodied, handsome and spirited horse.

The first time the King of Chu mounted the horse and began galloping, he felt the wind whizzing past his ears. In just a short time, he covered 100 *li*. Later, this 1000-*li* horse was credited with helping the King of Chu win many battles, and the King gained even greater respect for Bo Le.

The original parable about Bo Le, dating from over 2000 years ago, was created by scholars to illustrate a sad reality in political life: that talented people who perform brilliantly in their jobs often go unrecognized,

伯乐完成了使命,带着千里马直奔楚国。牵马到了楚王宫,伯乐拍着马的脖颈说:"我给你找到了好主人!"千里马好像明白了伯乐的意思,抬起前蹄嗑嗒嗑嗒地敲打着地面,仰天发出震耳欲聋的嘶鸣。楚王听到马嘶声,走到宫外来看看怎么一回事儿。伯乐指着千里马说:"大王请看,我给您带来了最好的千里马!"

看着面前这匹骨瘦如柴的马,楚王感到伯乐在愚弄他,于是很生气地说:"我相信你有识别好马的本事,才命你出去替我买马。可是你找来的是什么马啊?它看上去路都走不动,怎么能驰骋疆场呢?"伯乐冷静地给楚王解释说:"大王,这确实是一匹千里马。因为原来的主人一直用它来拉车,而且没有好好喂养,它才看上去骨瘦如柴。如果这匹马得到悉心喂养,不出半个月,就会成为一匹骏马。大王啊,我干嘛要骗你呢?"楚王虽然还有点半信半疑,但也感觉到伯乐很真诚,于是决定给这匹马一个机会证明自己。楚王命自己的马倌好好照顾这匹马,悉心喂养,让它恢复体力。对这匹马来说,此生第一次住进了天堂!不出所料,这个骨瘦如柴的家伙很快就成为了一匹健壮又神采奕奕的骏马。

楚王第一次骑上这匹千里马的时候,只觉得两耳生风,眨眼的工夫就跑出了一百里地。后来,这匹马为楚王赢得许多战役,立下了汗马功劳,而楚王也更加敬佩伯乐了。

这个寓言故事从两千多年前就流传开来。古代的思想家原来用它来比喻从政人士面对的一个可悲的现实。那就是一些原本可以在政治上大显身手的能人志士往往不被认

suffering misunderstanding and even abuse.* It takes a Bo Le to salvage such people from oblivion and give them a chance to realize their potential. Around 800 CE (during the Tang dynasty), a preamble was added to the story: "The world must first have a Bo Le, and only then can there be a 1000-*li* horse. 1000-*li* horses are common but a Bo Le is rare." This preamble introduced the following philosophical idea: While we may prize 1000-*li* horses, they are not so rare. What's really rare are the people who can recognize and nurture them. Today, the proverb "Bo Le appraises horses" is used primarily to express admiration for individuals who can recognize talent and provide opportunities for them.

---

* Chinese history is strewn with examples of heroes who were overlooked or abused by ignorant ill-advised emperors, from Han Feizi (author of the stories "Waiting for Rabbits by a Tree Stump" and "An Imposter in the Orchestra"), to Han Yu (author of this Bo Le story), to the modern-day Liu Shaoqi.

可,遭到误解,甚至虐待。*这样的能人志士需要伯乐来发现他们,给他们提供一个实现自我的机会。到了公元800年左右(唐朝),这个寓言故事的开头增加了这样一段话:"世界上先有伯乐,然后才有千里马,千里马很常见,而伯乐却不常见。"这段前言的深层意思是:尽管千里马很有价值,但并不少见;这个世界真正缺少的是能够发现千里马的人。今天,对那些能够发现并提携人才的人,人们往往用"伯乐相马"这个成语来表达他们的敬意。

The Chinese Proverb

伯	乐	相	马
Bó	**Lè**	**xiàng**	**mǎ**
Bo	Le	to appraise	a horse

Literal meaning: Bo Le appraises a horse.

Connotation: A "Bo Le" is an especially astute observer of talent who provides an opportunity for that talent to flourish.

The original source:

1. *Han's Exegeses on the Classic of Poetry*, Volume 7; by Han Ying (ca. 200–130 BCE), Han dynasty. 汉•韩婴(約前200–130年)《韩诗外传•卷七》
2. "Philosophy about Horses," by Han Yu (768–824), Tang dynasty. 唐•韩愈(公元768–824年),《马说》

---

* 中国历史上有很多这样的例子:很多能人志士因为皇帝昏庸或听信谗言而不被重用或遭到虐待,从"守株待兔"和"滥竽充数"的作者韩非子到"伯乐相马"的作者韩愈,以至于当代的刘少奇。

Vocabulary

1.	传说	chuánshuō	legend
2.	马匹	mǎpī	horses
3.	神仙	shénxiān	immortals
4.	命	mìng	to order (someone to do something)
5.	遍寻天下	biàn xún tiānxià	to search all over the world
6.	日行千里	rì xíng qiānlǐ	to run 1000 li a day
7.	骏马	jùnmǎ	excellent steed
8.	领命	lǐngmìng	to receive an order (to do something)
9.	耐心	nàixīn	to be patient
10.	等待	děngdài	to wait
11.	寻找	xúnzhǎo	to search for
12.	盛产	shèngchǎn	to produce in abundance
13.	良	liáng	superior
14.	盐	yán	salt
15.	陡坡	dǒupō	steep slope
16.	吃力	chīlì	laborious
17.	筋疲力尽	jīn pí lì jìn	to be totally exhausted
18.	气喘吁吁	qìchuǎn xūxū	huffing and puffing, out of breath
19.	睁	zhēng	to open the eyes wide
20.	仰天长啸	yǎngtiān chángxiào	to cry out at length to heaven
21.	倾诉	qīngsù	to pour out one's heart
22.	马嘶	mǎ sī	neighing of a horse
23.	断定	duàndìng	to determine, to diagnose
24.	赶车	gǎnchē	to drive a cart
25.	驰骋	chíchěng	to gallop
26.	疆场	jiāngchǎng	battlefield
27.	任何···都···	rènhé...dōu...	(used with a negative) none can ...
28.	却	què	but, and yet
29.	骨瘦如柴	gǔ shòu rú chái	bony as sticks of firewood
30.	傻瓜	shǎguā	an idiot, a fool
31.	合算	hésuàn	worthwhile, a good deal
32.	毫不	háobù	not in the least
33.	犹豫	yóuyù	to hesitate

34. 提议	tíyì	proposal
35. 使命	shǐmìng	mission
36. 直奔	zhíbèn	to rush straight toward
37. 牵	qiān	to lead (by a leash or rope)
38. 脖颈	bójǐng	back of the neck
39. 前蹄	qiántí	front hooves
40. 嗑嗒嗑嗒	kēdākēdā	sound of tapping or pounding
41. 敲打	qiāodǎ	to pound on
42. 震耳欲聋	zhèn ěr yù lóng	deafening, extremely loud
43. 嘶鸣	sīmíng	braying of a horse
44. 愚弄	yúnòng	to deceive, to make a fool of (someone)
45. 识别	shíbié	to distinguish, to discern
46. 本事	běnshi	ability
47. 冷静	lěngjìng	calm and cool
48. 喂养	wèiyǎng	to feed and raise (animal)
49. 悉心	xīxīn	with utmost care
50. 半信半疑	bànxìn bànyí	half-believing and half-doubting
51. 马倌	mǎguān	a groom, person in charge of horses
52. 恢复	huīfù	to recover
53. 此生	cǐshēng	in this life
54. 天堂	tiāntáng	heaven
55. 不出所料	bù chū suǒ liào	as expected
56. 家伙	jiāhuo	guy, fellow (colloquial)
57. 健壮	jiànzhuàng	healthy and strong
58. 神采奕奕	shéncǎi yìyì	beaming with high spirits
59. 两耳生风	liǎng'ěr shēngfēng	wind whizzing by both ears (i.e., moving fast)
60. 眨眼的工夫	zhǎyǎnde gōngfu	in a blink, in a brief moment
61. 赢得	yíngdé	to win, to attain victory
62. 战役	zhànyì	campaign, battle
63. 汗马功劳	hànmǎ gōngláo	distinctive merit
64. 敬佩	jìngpèi	admiration, esteem
65. 寓言故事	yùyán gùshi	parable
66. 流传	liúchuán	to circulate

67.	比喻	**bǐyù**	metaphor, analogy; to draw an analogy
68.	从政	**cóngzhèng**	to engage in politics or government service
69.	可悲	**kěbēi**	sad, lamentable
70.	现实	**xiànshí**	reality
71.	大显身手	**dà xiǎn shēnshǒu**	to display one's skills to the fullest
72.	能人志士	**néngrén zhìshì**	capable and ambitious person
73.	认可	**rènkě**	to approve

....

The Proverb in Modern Usage

Recruiting Superb Language Teachers

If I may say so myself, I have been quite successful as a professor of Chinese. However, my greatest accomplishment is to have been a "Bo Le" who discovered a number of "1000-*li* horses" in China. My claim to success is proven by the fact that these "1000-*li* horses" have become eminent Chinese language teachers in the U.S. When China opened up to the world in the 1980s, I had the opportunity to direct study-abroad programs for American students in China, so I was in the perfect position to be a talent scout for Chinese language teachers. Teaching a foreign language is not just about teaching the language, but also about being a bridge to a foreign culture. It requires much more than linguistic knowledge and the ability to convey that knowledge. A good language teacher must have good interpersonal skills, be culturally sensitive, empathetic and able to inspire students to be eager learners. As time has proven, I have been a good judge of these precious personality traits. As I think back on my own experience as an accidental Bo Le, I cannot totally agree with the view that "1000-*li* horses are common, but a Bo Le is rare." There are legions of Chinese language teachers now but "1000-*li* horses" are not that common, whereas a Bo Le may simply be a good observer of human nature who happens to be at the right place and the right time to encounter exceptional "1000-*li* horses."

74. 遭到	**zāodào**	to meet with (misfortune)
75. 误解	**wùjiě**	misunderstanding
76. 虐待	**nüèdài**	abuse, maltreatment
77. 深层	**shēncéng**	deep level
78. 提携	**tíxié**	to guide and support
79. 敬意	**jìngyì**	respect, esteem
80. 昏庸	**hūnyōng**	stupid, foolish
81. 谗言	**chányán**	slander

成语今用实例

发掘汉语教师千里马

不是自夸，我在中文教学这个行业里算是挺成功的，但是我自认为最大的成就是在中国发现了一小批"千里马"。证明我不是自吹自擂的依据就是这些"千里马"如今已成为了美国汉语教学领域的优秀教师。中国在八十年代开始对外开放的时候，我就有机会在中国担任美国汉语留学项目的负责人，因此我处在最佳的位置来寻找中文教师人才。教外语并不只是简单地教一门语言，而是要在文化上起到桥梁的作用。因此，一名优秀的语言教师不仅要掌握语言方面的知识以及具备传授知识的能力，还应该有良好的人际沟通能力，在文化方面有敏感度，能跟他人产生共鸣，以及具备激发学生学习兴趣的能力。实事求是地说，我很善于发现他人身上这些宝贵的个人品质。回顾我偶然成为伯乐的个人经历，我并不完全同意"千里马很常见，而伯乐却不常见"的说法。现在对外汉语教学领域已经有众多的教师，但"千里马"并不那么多；而"伯乐"只不过是一个善于观察人性的普通人，在恰当的时间和恰当的地点有幸遇到一些千里马。

Vocabulary

82.	发掘	**fājué**	to discover, to excavate
83.	自夸	**zìkuā**	to brag
84.	行业	**hángyè**	professional field
85.	成就	**chéngjiù**	accomplishment
86.	批	**pī**	batch
87.	自吹自擂	**zìchuī zìléi**	to blow one's own horn
88.	依据	**yījù**	evidence, basis
89.	领域	**lǐngyù**	field
90.	优秀	**yōuxiù**	superior
91.	担任	**dānrèn**	to serve in the capacity of
92.	项目	**xiàngmù**	program, project
93.	处在	**chǔzài**	to be situated at/in
94.	最佳	**zuìjiā**	best, most advantageous
95.	位置	**wèizhi**	position
96.	起···作用	**qǐ...zuòyòng**	to have the effect of ..., to bring about...
97.	桥梁	**qiáoliáng**	bridge
98.	以及	**yǐjí**	and, moreover
99.	具备	**jùbèi**	to have, to be equipped with...
100.	传授	**chuánshòu**	to transmit (knowledge)
101.	人际沟通	**rénjì gōutōng**	interpersonal communication
102.	敏感度	**mǐn'gǎndù**	sensitivity
103.	共鸣	**gòngmíng**	resonance, sympathetic response
104.	激发	**jīfā**	to arouse, to stimulate
105.	实事求是	**shíshì qiúshì**	to be practical and realistic
106.	善于	**shànyú**	to be good at
107.	品质	**pǐnzhì**	quality, character
108.	回顾	**huígù**	to look back on, to view in retrospect
109.	偶然	**ǒurán**	fortuitous, by chance
110.	众多	**zhòngduō**	multitude
111.	观察	**guānchá**	to observe

| 112. 恰当 | qiàdàng | appropriate, suitable |
| 113. 有幸 | yǒuxìng | to have the good fortune of ... |

Discussion questions (discuss in English or Chinese):

1. Have you known someone who could be called a "1000-*li* horse" or a "Bo Le" in your life? In your opinion, which is harder to come by in our contemporary society?

2. If a manager in your company who has been the company's "1000-*li* horse" for the last ten years is about to retire, how would you go about finding a replacement? Would you trust an HR firm to be the "Bo Le" in that search?

3. If you have not heard of Jack Ma, look him up on the internet before proceeding with this question. A number of brilliant "1000-*li* horses" in modern China are known to have been quashed by the Chinese college entrance exam system. The total number of these "1000-*li* horses" is unknown because the ones who fall into oblivion are unaccounted for. The best success story might be Jack Ma, founder of Alibaba. He failed the annual college entrance exam four times before he finally got admitted to a second-rate college. Harvard Business School also rejected him 10 times. He was repeatedly rejected for the many lowly jobs that he applied for. And yet he became one of the most successful entrepreneurs in China. So the question is, how can the many other "1000-*li* horses" in modern China gain recognition, aside from a chance meeting with a Bo Le?

Planning Lies with Man, But Success Lies with Heaven

The history of the Three Kingdoms period (220–280 CE)* is familiar to everyone in China, because it was a legendary era filled with famous cultural heroes. But what most Chinese know derive from the semi-fictional novel *Romance of the Three Kingdoms* rather than from historical records. To the present day, the stories of many heroes from this period appear in movies, TV programs and even computer games, so they are well known. The Chinese proverb "planning lies with man, but success lies with heaven" originated with one of the many stories from the Three Kingdoms period.

Near the end of the Han dynasty, China split into three regions controlled by warlords, which eventually became the kingdoms of Wei, Shu and Wu. Roughly speaking, Wei was in the north, Shu was in the west (present-day Sichuan Province), and Wu was in the southeast. Relations among these three kingdoms were sometimes peaceful and sometimes not. Whenever a relationship turned tense, war would break out.

---

* The dates 220–280 CE for the Three Kingdoms period are somewhat arbitrary, because historians don't all agree on which historical events should be used to mark the beginning and end of the era. In fact, many of the legends associated with the Three Kingdoms period date back to around 184 CE, when the Han dynasty began to disintegrate into many regions controlled by warlords, of which three emerged as supreme by 220 CE. The term "kingdoms" in "Three Kingdoms" is also a bit of a misnomer. Although the rulers of the Three Kingdoms each controlled only one of the three regions of China, all of them claimed to be the legitimate emperor of all of China—not just a king. The territories under the three regimes also changed within the span of sixty years. The map on the opposite page represents the status as of 238 CE.

谋事在人，成事在天

一提起三国 (220–280)，中国人都知道那是一个<u>人才济济</u>，<u>英雄辈出</u>的时代。然而中国老百姓对那个时代的了解大多来自半<u>虚构</u>的小说《<u>三国演义</u>》而不是<u>正史</u>。直到今天，许多历史<u>风云人物</u>和他们的故事仍然为人们<u>耳熟能详</u>，<u>津津乐道</u>，也成为电影、电视，甚至电脑游戏的题材。"谋事在人，成事在天"这个<u>谚语</u>就是出自三国的一个历史故事。

汉朝末年，中国出现了三王<u>争霸</u>的<u>局面</u>，就是后来的魏、蜀、吴三国。<u>大致</u>地说，魏国在中国的北方，蜀国在西南，也就是今天的四川一带，而吴国则在东南部。这三个国家之间的关系时好时坏，而关系紧张的时候就会打仗。

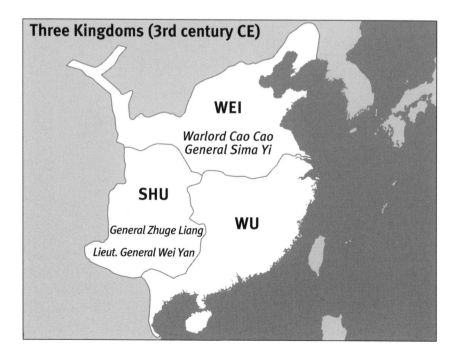

Three Kingdoms (3rd century CE)

WEI

Warlord Cao Cao
General Sima Yi

SHU

General Zhuge Liang
Lieut. General Wei Yan

WU

All three kingdoms had capable generals as well as brilliant military counselors who masterminded strategies for their kings. Zhuge Liang was the military counselor for the king of Shu. To the Chinese, he is the ultimate embodiment of wisdom. Many stories about him could be called myths and some were in fact folklore that developed in later times.

One example is the story of Zhuge Liang "borrowing the east wind" in battle. In the winter of 208–209, when the three regions were struggling for supremacy, the two warlords in the south joined forces to engage the northern warlord Cao Cao in a naval battle on the Yangtze River at a place called Red Cliff. After everything was readied for battle, Zhuge Liang realized that he would have to wait for the direction of the wind to change to his advantage. The wind blows from the northwest for most of the winter, but being an expert in meteorology, Zhuge Liang calculated that it would soon turn to be from the east for a spell. To get the full charismatic effect, he stood up on an altar to summon the east wind. Sure enough, he succeeded in "borrowing" the east wind and defeated Cao Cao's forces. The proverb "all is ready except the east wind" comes from this story.

三个国家都有许多能打仗的将军，也有很多给国王出谋划策的聪明军师。诸葛亮就是蜀国的军师。对中国人来说，诸葛亮是智慧的化身；有关他的很多故事都称得上传奇，有的甚至于是后来民间创作出来的传说。

　　比方说，"借东风"的故事。公元208-209年的冬天，魏、蜀、吴三国还在相互争霸。有一次，蜀国和吴国联合起来，跟魏王曹操在长江上一个叫赤壁的地方交战。一切都准备好了，可是突然发现那天的风向不利于他们水上作战。诸葛亮意识到必须等风向改变才能开战。一般来说，那里的冬天常刮西北风。但是精通天象的诸葛亮已经看出来了，风向马上会转成东风。于是，诸葛亮就像神一样，在祭坛上呼风唤雨，借来了东风，跟吴国一起打败了魏国。中文里"万事俱备，只欠东风"就来自这个故事。

General Sima Yi of the kingdom of Wei, a contemporary of Zhuge Liang, was another famous person from the Three Kingdoms era. He was a prodigy who showed exceptional resourcefulness and ingenuity from a young age. At the age of forty he became the tutor for the crown prince of Wei. When that prince became king, he elevated Sima Yi to the position of royal advisor and military strategist, and Sima Yi led the Wei army through many successful campaigns. In one battle, a general from Shu thought that Sima Yi's army was still quite far away and it would take another month before the enemy would arrive. What he failed to foresee was that Sima Yi could motivate his men to march day and night, and reach the Shu encampment in just eight days. Taken by surprise, the Shu forces were wiped out and the general was captured alive. This one episode alone made it obvious that Sima Yi was a general of extraordinary leadership ability.

Zhuge Liang and Sima Yi had faced each other in many military contests and each knew full-well that his opponent was no easy match. At the battle of Celestial Valley (a fictitious place concocted by the author of *Romance of the Three Kingdoms*), Zhuge Liang thought he finally had the perfect opportunity to annihilate Sima Yi. In the spring of 234, with an army of 350,000 men, Zhuge Liang prepared to face Sima Yi's army of 400,000 in a life-or-death battle. He first surveyed the lay of the land and saw that Celestial Valley was flanked by two mountains that came close together at the end, thus forming a narrow exit from the valley. He immediately hatched a brilliant plot.

Zhuge Liang first sent his general Wei Yan to engage Sima Yi in battle, and instructed Wei Yan to allow Sima Yi's forces to defeat him. Wei Yan's forces were then to retreat in the direction of Celestial Valley, thereby luring Sima Yi's pursuing army into the valley. Although Sima Yi was extremely clever, this time he really thought he had defeated the Shu forces. As his army chased Wei Yan's division into the valley, suddenly there was a loud explosion, followed by an avalanche of rocks and wood which effectively blocked the exit from the valley. Next came an avalanche of torches tossed by Shu soldiers from above, which instantly ignited the firewood and explosives that had been laid in advance on the valley floor. Soon the valley turned into a blazing inferno. Sima Yi, realizing that he had fallen for Zhuge Liang's trap, thought he was headed for a quick and certain death.

魏国的大将军司马懿跟诸葛亮是同一个历史时期的名人。司马懿从小聪明过人，很年轻的时候就表现出来了足智多谋的才能。40岁那年，司马懿成为了魏国皇太子的老师。后来皇太子成了皇帝，就重用司马懿，而司马懿也为魏王献计献策，并带领魏国的军队立下了很多战功。有一次，司马懿与蜀国的一个将军打仗。蜀国将军以为司马懿的军队离得很远，骑马行军至少要一个月才能跟他们交战。没想到司马懿带领军队日夜兼程，只用了八天就到了蜀国军队驻扎的地方，出其不意地击败了蜀国的军队，还活捉了蜀国将军。由此可见，司马懿的领导能力非同一般。

诸葛亮跟司马懿当然较量过很多次，因而彼此都深知对方不好对付。在上方谷（是《三国演义》作者假想的地方），诸葛亮认为他终于等到了歼灭司马懿的绝好机会。公元234年的春天，诸葛亮带蜀兵35万人，而司马懿带魏兵40万人，准备决一死战。有一天，诸葛亮查看了地形以后，发现上方谷两边是高山，山谷里有一块低地，谷口很窄，他马上想到了一条妙计。

诸葛亮派蜀国大将军魏延去挑战司马懿，并且告诉魏延只准败不准胜，最后要把司马懿和他的兵马一步一步地引诱进上方谷。尽管司马懿很狡猾，但这次他真的以为蜀国兵马被打败了，就一路追赶进了上方谷。突然一声炮响，山上滚下来一些石头木头，把谷口堵住了。接着山上的蜀国士兵又扔下来一些火把，点燃了事先在谷底埋下的干柴，火药。上方谷顿时成了一片火海，这时司马懿才意识到自己上了诸葛亮的当，以为自己这次死定了！

Zhuge Liang was ecstatic to see the flames rising from the valley and thought that he had finally destroyed Sima Yi. At that moment, however, a strong wind whipped up, followed by a torrential downpour, which extinguished the flames. Sima Yi's grief immediately turned to joy. He looked up and shouted: "Heaven did not let us die! If we don't run now, what are we waiting for?" The Wei army spurred their horses, and with lightning speed made their escape from Celestial Valley. From the top of the mountain, Zhuge Liang realized that his brilliant scheme had just been foiled by a torrential rain. In resignation, he gazed up at heaven, let out a long sigh, and uttered the proverbial words "Planning lies with man, but success lies with heaven!"

The Chinese proverb

谋	事	在	人,	成	事	在	天!
móu	shì	zài	rén,	chéng	shì	zài	tiān
to plan	matters	lies with	man,	to succeed	matters	lies with	Heaven

Literal meaning: Planning lies with man, but success lies with heaven.

Connotation: A mortal human being may lay ingenious plans and exert great efforts, but success depends on factors beyond his control.

The original source: Romance of the Three Kingdoms, a 14th century historical novel attributed to Luo Guanzhong 罗贯中 《三国演义》

诸葛亮看着上方谷里的熊熊大火，心里大喜，以为这次总算把司马懿干掉了。正在这个时候，突然刮起了大风，下起了大雨，很快把大火扑灭了。司马懿立刻转悲为喜，仰天大叫："天不亡我，此时不逃，更待何时？"说完扬鞭策马，杀出一条血路，逃出了上方谷。诸葛亮在山上看到他精心设计的计划因为一场大雨而泡汤了，也只能仰天长叹一声："谋事在人，成事在天！"

Vocabulary

1.	人才济济	réncái jǐjǐ	an abundance of talented people
2.	英雄辈出	yīngxióng bèichū	a large number of heroes
3.	虚构	xūgòu	to fictionalize, to fabricate
4.	三国演义	Sānguó Yǎnyì	*History of the Three Kingdoms*
5.	正史	zhèngshǐ	standard history
6.	风云人物	fēngyún rénwù	influential individuals
7.	耳熟能详	ér-shú-néng-xiáng	frequently heard and able to recite in detail
8.	津津乐道	jīnjīn lèdào	to take delight in talking about
9.	谚语	yànyǔ	proverb, common saying
10.	争霸	zhēngbà	to vie for supremacy
11.	局面	júmiàn	situation
12.	大致	dàzhì	roughly, on the whole, more or less
13.	出谋划策	chūmóu huàcè	to come up with great strategies
14.	军师	jūnshī	military general
15.	智慧	zhìhuì	wisdom

16.	化身	huàshēn	incarnate, embodiment
17.	称得上	chēngdeshàng	can be called
18.	传奇	chuánqí	legend
19.	赤壁	Chì Bì	Red Cliff
20.	交战	jiāozhàn	to engage in battle
21.	不利于...	búlìyú...	to be disadvantageous for ...
22.	刮…风	guā...fēng	blowing of the wind (from a certain direction)
23.	精通	jīngtōng	to be an expert in
24.	天象	tiānxiàng	meteorology
25.	祭坛	jìtán	sacrificial altar
26.	呼风唤雨	hūfēng huànyǔ	to call to the wind and rain
27.	万事俱备，只欠东风	wànshì jù bèi, zhǐ qiàn dōngfēng	everything is ready, only lacking the east wind
28.	…过人	… guòrén	surpassing others in ..., exceptional in...
29.	足智多谋	zúzhì duōmóu	full of wisdom and ideas, resourceful
30.	重用	zhòngyòng	to assign to important tasks
31.	献计献策	xiànjì xiàncè	to come up with great plans and strategies
32.	立下…战功	lìxià...zhàngōng	to render meritorious service in battle
33.	日夜兼程	rìyè jiān chéng	on the road day and night
34.	驻扎	zhùzhā	to be stationed (re troops)
35.	出其不意	chū qí búyì	to be taken by surprise
36.	击败	jībài	to defeat, to vanquish
37.	活捉	huózhuō	to capture alive
38.	由此可见	yóu cǐ kě jiàn	it can be seen from this
39.	非同一般	fēi tóng yìbān	out of the ordinary
40.	较量	jiàoliàng	to have a contest (with an opponent)
41.	对付	duìfu	to deal with (a rival or adversary)
42.	假想	jiǎxiǎng	imagined, hypothetical, fictitious
43.	歼灭	jiānmiè	to annihilate, to wipe out

44.	绝好	juéhǎo	extremely good
45.	决一死战	jué-yī-sǐ-zhàn	to fight a life-and-death battle
46.	妙计	miàojì	brilliant scheme
47.	挑战	tiǎozhàn	to pick a battle, to challenge
48.	引诱	yǐnyòu	to lure, to entice
49.	狡猾	jiǎohuá	cunning
50.	追赶	zhuīgǎn	to chase after
51.	炮响	pàoxiǎng	the boom of canons
52.	火把	huǒbǎ	torch
53.	点燃	diǎnrán	to ignite
54.	干柴	gānchái	dry firewood
55.	火药	huǒyào	explosives
56.	顿时	dùnshí	at once
57.	上…当	shàng...dàng	to fall for so-and-so's trick, to be fooled by…
58.	熊熊大火	xióngxióng dàhuǒ	big blazing fire
59.	干掉	gàndiào	(slang) to get rid of, to liquidate
60.	扑灭	pūmiè	to extinguish (a fire)
61.	转悲为喜	zhuǎn bēi wéi xǐ	to turn sorrow into joy
62.	仰天	yǎngtiān	to look up at heaven
63.	天不亡我， 此时不逃， 更待何时	tiān bù wáng wǒ, cǐ shí bù táo, gèng dài hé shí	heaven did not let me die, if I don't escape now, what am I waiting for?
64.	扬鞭策马	yáng biān cè mǎ	to raise the whip to spur the horse
65.	杀出…血路	shāchū...xuèlù	to cut a desperate escape route
66.	精心	jīngxīn	painstakingly, meticulously
67.	泡汤	pàotāng	to come to nothing (lit. "to soak in broth")
68.	长叹一声	chángtàn yìshēng	to let out a long sigh

Chasing Your Dreams

The present generation of talented young people—despite their natural abilities and strong efforts—have no guarantees that they will realize their dreams. For example, a first-generation college student may dream of returning to her poverty-ridden hometown to found a school, and may prepare herself for this mission through sustained hard work. But whether or not she can achieve her dream is not determined solely by herself, as she has no control over certain other factors, what the Chinese call "heaven's will." Therefore, if carefully laid plans fail in the end, we can comfort ourselves with the proverb "planning lies with man but success lies with heaven," and free ourselves from regrets.

Discussion questions (discuss in English or Chinese):

1. Another common saying that involves the legendary Zhuge Liang is 三个臭皮匠顶个诸葛亮 **sānge chòu píjiàng dǐng ge Zhūgě Liàng** "Three stinky cobblers can outdo one Zhuge Liang)." This one is especially applicable to present-day scenarios. Find out what it means and think of a scenario in which you would use it.

2. The Battle of Red Cliff (associated with the proverb 万事俱备，只欠东风 **wànshì jùbèi, zhǐ qiàn dōngfēng** "All is ready, only lacking the east wind" cited in this story) has become well-known globally through the movie Red Cliff. The legendary version (based on a chapter in *Romance of the Three Kingdoms*) deviates from history quite a bit. You may read about the movie and the history on the internet. As of this writing, these two sources were still accessible:

   https://en.wikipedia.org/wiki/Battle_of_Red_Cliffs
   https://en.wikipedia.org/wiki/Red_Cliff_(film)

   Compare the two versions to see an example of how history is transformed into legends. You may also enjoy the movie Red Cliff, which is available on Amazon Prime Video.

3. For additional entertainment, and to stretch your Chinese comprehension ability, ask any Chinese friend to tell you their favorite stories from the Three Kingdoms period.

第一代大学生的梦想

生活在今天的年轻人，尽管非常聪明努力，最终还是有可能实现不了自己的<u>梦想</u>。<u>譬如</u>，一个第一代大学生的梦想就是毕业以后回<u>贫困</u>的故乡办学校，因此努力学习，积极准备。然而，这个学生的梦想<u>能否</u>实现还不是他自己能决定的，还有许多其他<u>不可控</u>的<u>因素</u>，也就是我们说的"<u>天意</u>"。因此，如果一个人精心设计的计划最后没有成功，可以用"谋事在人，成事在天！"这个谚语来<u>安慰</u>自己，这样就没有<u>遗憾</u>了。

Vocabulary

69.	梦想	**mèngxiǎng**	dream, fervent hope
70.	譬如	**pìrú**	for example
71.	贫困	**pínkùn**	poor, impoverished
72.	能否	**néngfǒu**	to be able to or not
73.	不可控	**bùkě kòng**	cannot be controlled
74.	因素	**yīnsù**	factor
75.	天意	**tiānyì**	will of heaven
76.	安慰	**ānwèi**	to comfort, to console
77.	遗憾	**yíhàn**	regret

Azure Blue Is from Indigo But Surpasses Indigo

A well-known aspect of traditional Chinese culture is respect for teachers. And yet, the Chinese have invented the proverb in the title of this story to honor students who surpass their teachers while preserving the dignity of the teachers. This reciprocal relationship between teacher and student is illustrated by the following true story.

Near the end of the late Northern Wei dynasty (ca. 500 CE) there was a famous teacher by the name of Kong Fan. Not only was he the most learned man of his time, but his character was also impeccable. Instead of being ambitious about his own advancement, he was dedicated to the advancement of his students. Among his many outstanding students was a prodigy by the name of Li Mi. By age 13, Li Mi had already mastered all the classics of philosophy, art and science. At age 18, he beseeched Kong Fan to be his mentor in order to gain a deeper understanding of the classics. Li Mi not only learned everything that Kong Fan taught him, but he could also think outside the box and synthesize new knowledge with the old. In just a few short years, Kong Fan realized that Li Mi had surpassed him and he was delighted to see this level of development in his pupil.

One day Kong Fan encountered a conundrum and he had no mentor to go to, so he decided to seek advice from his pupil Li Mi. Up to this point, Li Mi had always interacted with his mentor with utmost deference, so he was caught off guard and didn't know how to respond. Kong Fan sensed his embarrassment, so he quickly added, "There's nothing to be embarrassed about. Even a sage can learn from others, let alone a teacher like me! Anyone who has some knowledge that I lack, I consider to be my teacher, and that includes you!" When word got out that Kong Fan humbled himself to seek advice from one of his pupils, all his other pupils were so excited that they composed a little ditty to extol this spirit of learning from those beneath one's rank:

青出于蓝，而胜于蓝

在中国传统文化中，尊师是很重要的一个观念。然而，这篇文章的标题采用的成语，既赞美了学问超越老师的学生，同时也维护了老师的尊严。下面这个真实的故事就完美地诠释了师生之间这种教学相长的关系。

北魏末年(约公元500年)有一位很有名的老师，名叫孔璠。他不但是那个时代最有学问的人，人品也完美无瑕。作为老师，孔璠不是为自己成名成家，而是全身心地致力于培养学生。在许多优秀的学生当中，有一位名叫李谧的神童。李谧十三岁的时候，就已经通读了哲学、艺术以及科学的所有经典著述。李谧十八岁那年，恳切地拜孔璠为师，以求对文史哲的经典著述有更深入的理解。李谧不但掌握了孔璠传授给他的一切知识，而且并不墨守成规，时常温故知新，融会贯通。仅仅几年的时间里，孔璠就意识到李谧已经超越了自己，并为有这样出色的弟子而感到十分欣慰。

有一天，孔璠遇到了一个让他迷惑不解的难题，而又没有老师可以求教，于是就决定请教自己的学生李谧。一直以来，李谧对老师都毕恭毕敬，因此，老师突然来向他求教，倒让他一下子不知道怎么回应才好。见李谧很不自在的样子，孔璠连忙说："没事儿，连圣人都会向别人学习，何况我呢！谁有我所没有的知识，我就应该拜他为师，这也包括你呀！"孔璠不耻下问，向学生求教的事情传开来以后，他的弟子们都非常惊喜，大家编了一首小歌谣，赞美这样一种不耻下问的精神。小歌谣是这样写的：

Azure blue comes from indigo,
Yet indigo bows to azure blue.
What is always true about a teacher?
He is the one who can explain the classics!

The first time the relationship between "azure" and "indigo" was used metaphorically was around 250 BCE, in the following essay by the philosopher Xunzi on the value of education.

Azure is derived from indigo but it is superior to indigo; ice is made from water but it is colder than water; wood can be bent to form a wheel while it is still supple; a sheet of metal becomes a blade when it is honed ...

The message in Xunzi's essay was that a common person can be transformed by education. This may have been a novel idea in Xunzi's time, but it has long become a commonly accepted truism. It was more than seven centuries after Xunzi that Kong Fan's pupils wrote that ditty to tease their teacher, but due to this event, the relationship between "azure" and "indigo" was given a new twist that made it a favorite proverb to this day.

"青成蓝，蓝谢青，师何常，在明经。"意思就是"青
色出自蓝靛，而蓝靛不如青色。世上没有固定的老
师，谁通晓经典谁就是老师。"

大约在公元前250年，古代哲学家荀子在一篇谈论教育的
文章里，首次谈到了"蓝"和"青"的关系。

青，取之于蓝而青于蓝；冰，水为之而寒于水；木
直中绳，輮以为轮；金就砺则利…

荀子在文章里告诉大家，教育可以将一个普通人变成
有用之才。在荀子生活的时代，那样的想法或许算得上很新
奇，但在今天早已是人尽皆知的共识了。荀子之后又过了七
百多年，孔璠的弟子们写歌谣调侃老师的时候，"蓝"与"青"
之间的关系有了新的寓意，使"青出于蓝而胜于蓝"成为了今
天最常用的成语之一。

The Chinese proverb

青	出	于	蓝,	而	胜	于	蓝
qīng	chū	yú	lán,	ér	shèng	yú	lán
azure	emerges	from	indigo,	but	surpasses	over	indigo

Literal meaning: The color blue comes from indigo (the plant) but is superior to indigo.

Connotation: An outstanding student is produced by the teacher, but has surpassed the teacher.

The original source:
1. "Advice on Learning," an essay by Xunzi (313–238 BCE) 《荀子•劝学》（公元前313–238年）
2. *History of the Wei Dynasty*, Vol. 90, "Biographies of Virtuous Men," section 78. By Wei Shou (506–572) of the Northern Qi dynasty 魏书卷九十，列传逸士第七十八。作者: 北齐•魏收(506–572年)

Vocabulary

1.	尊师	**zūnshī**	respect for teachers
2.	观念	**guānniàn**	concept
3.	标题	**biāotí**	title
4.	采用	**cǎiyòng**	to adopt for use
5.	既…也…	**jì...yě...**	both ... and ...
6.	赞美	**zànměi**	to praise
7.	超越	**chāoyuè**	to surpass
8.	维护	**wéihù**	to safeguard, to uphold
9.	尊严	**zūnyán**	dignity
10.	完美	**wánměi**	perfect
11.	诠释	**quánshì**	to expound, to interpret
12.	教学相长	**jiāoxué xiāngzhǎng**	teaching and learning enhance mutual development
13.	人品	**rénpǐn**	personal character
14.	无瑕	**wúxiá**	flawless (often combined with 完美, as in 完美无瑕)
15.	不是…而是…	**búshì...érshì...**	it is not ..., but it is ...
16.	成名成家	**chéngmíng chéngjiā**	to make a name for oneself
17.	致力于	**zhìlìyú**	to devote one's efforts toward ...
18.	培养	**péiyǎng**	to cultivate
19.	优秀	**yōuxiù**	outstanding
20.	神童	**shéntóng**	prodigy
21.	通读	**tōngdú**	to have achieved mastery through study
22.	经典	**jīngdiǎn**	classic
23.	著述	**zhùshù**	written works
24.	恳切	**kěnqiè**	earnest, sincere
25.	拜…为师	**bài...wéi shī**	to humbly submit oneself to the tutelage of ... (a master)
26.	文史哲	**wén shǐ zhé**	literature, history, philosophy
27.	掌握	**zhǎngwò**	to have mastered, to have grasped

28.	传授	chuánshòu	to impart (knowledge)
29.	墨守成规	mòshǒu chéngguī	to stick to conventions
30.	温故知新	wēngù zhīxīn	to learn something new by reviewing something old
31.	融会贯通	rónghuì guàntōng	to master something by synthesizing disparate knowledge
32.	意识到	yìshidào	to realize, to become aware of
33.	出色	chūsè	outstanding, remarkable
34.	弟子	dìzǐ	pupil, disciple
35.	欣慰	xīnwèi	to be gratified
36.	迷惑不解	míhuò bùjiě	perplexed
37.	毕恭毕敬	bìgōng bìjìng	extremely deferential
38.	回应	huíyìng	to respond
39.	不自在	búzìzài	to be ill at ease
40.	连忙	liánmáng	promptly
41.	圣人	shèngrén	sage
42.	何况	hékuàng	let alone ...
43.	不耻下问	bùchǐ xiàwèn	to not be ashamed to ask a subordinate
44.	传开来	chuánkāilái	(re news) to spread around
45.	编	biān	to compose
46.	歌谣	gēyáo	folk song, ballad
47.	蓝靛	lándiàn	indigo
48.	固定	gùdìng	fixed, immutable
49.	通晓	tōngxiǎo	to be well-versed in something
50.	首次	shǒucì	the first time
51.	取之于	qǔ zhī yú	to be taken from, to arise from
52.	青于	qīngyú	bluer than ...
53.	寒于	hányú	colder than ...
54.	木直中绳，鞣以为轮	mù zhí zhòngshéng, róu yǐ wéi lún	wood can be perfectly straight, but it can be bent to form a wheel
55.	金就砺则利	jīn jiù lì zé lì	a piece of metal becomes sharp when honed by a whetstone

56. 才	cái	talent, a capable person
57. 新奇	xīnqí	novel
58. 人尽皆知	rén jìn jiē zhī	known to everyone

....

Leonardo Da Vinci and Maya Lin

For human civilization to advance, it is necessary for some students in each generation to surpass their teachers. In fact, the hallmark of a teacher's success is having many students who exemplify "azure emerging from indigo." Nowhere is this truer than in the arts, because becoming an artist is not just about acquiring knowledge and skills; it is first and foremost about having artistic talent.

One notable example is Leonardo Da Vinci and his master Verrocchio, a leading Florentine painter and sculptor in the 15th century. Leonardo began his career at age 14 as an apprentice in Verrocchio's studio. Within ten years, his paintings had equaled or surpassed those of his master. As the story goes, Verrocchio had Leonardo collaborate with him on his painting *The Baptism of Christ* and Leonardo painted the angel holding Jesus' robe. Verrocchio felt that this angel was so superior to his own work that he put down his brush and never painted again.[*]

---

[*] This story is one among several similar stories, and any of them may be apocryphal. But the implication of all these stories is based on reality.

59. 共识	**gòngshí**	common understanding, consensus
60. 调侃	**tiáokǎn**	to tease, to mock
61. 寓意	**yùyì**	allusion, implication

成语今用实例

达芬奇与林璎

人类文明要进步，就需要一代又一代人当中涌现出超越老师的优秀学子。事实上，能够带出一批"青出于蓝"的学生正是一位杰出教师的标志。从这个角度来看，艺术界比其他任何一个领域都更能证明这一点。要成为一位艺术家，一个人需要的不仅是掌握知识和技巧，最重要的是要有艺术天赋。

达芬奇与他的导师维洛及欧就是一个很好的例子。维洛及欧是十五世纪在佛罗伦斯最知名的画家与雕塑家，而达芬奇的艺术生涯始于十四岁那年开始在维洛及欧的画室里当一名学徒。在十年的时间里，达芬奇的画作就可以跟导师的媲美，甚至超过了导师的作品。据说，维洛及欧让达芬奇跟他一起合作，绘制"耶稣受洗"这幅画，而达芬奇画的是手持耶稣衣袍的天使。维洛及欧感觉到达芬奇画的天使远比自己的作品优秀，因而放下了画笔，从此不再作画了。*

---

* 这一类的故事有好几个版本，有可能都是虚构的，但这些故事所传达的寓意却是来自史实。

Another example closer to our time is Maya Lin, designer of the Vietnam Veterans Memorial in Washington D.C. In 1981, when the planning for this memorial was underway, a competition was held to select its design. The entries were judged anonymously by a jury of eight experts. Maya Lin, a senior at Yale at the time, beat out 1420 other competitors, including many accomplished architects and one of her own professors at Yale. The surprising thing was that Lin's design began as an assignment for a course at Yale, for which she only received a B! When the selected design was announced, it immediately became controversial, and Lin's design was severely criticized in some quarters. Ironically, one stipulation of the competition was that the designs had to be apolitical, yet politics ended up at the root of the controversies surrounding Lin's design. Reflecting on these controversies some years later, Lin wrote, "From the very beginning, I often wondered, if it had not been anonymous entry #1026 but rather an entry by Maya Lin, would my design have been selected?" Today Maya Lin is not only a renowned architect, but her portrait hangs in the National Portrait Gallery in Washington, D.C., and the Vietnam Veterans Memorial has become the most personally engaging landmark in the U.S. capital.[*]

---

[*] https://www.biography.com/news/maya-lin-vietnam-veterans-memorial

另外一个例子距离我们今天并不太遥远，那就是华盛顿特区越战纪念碑的设计者林璎。1981年，越战纪念碑正在筹建中的时候，就纪念碑的设计举办了一次竞赛。所有参赛的设计图将由一个八位专家组成的评委会来进行匿名评审。当时还是耶鲁大学本科四年级学生的林璎，击败了其他1420位竞赛选手，其中有不少相当有名气的设计师，还包括一位她在耶鲁大学的教授。令人惊讶的是，林璎的参赛作品原本是她在耶鲁大学一门课的作业，而这幅设计作品她只得到了B的成绩！林璎的中选设计图一公布，立即引起了争议，并遭到某些人士的激烈批评。具有讽刺意味的是，此次竞赛的一项规定是设计作品必须不带任何政治色彩，而政治却恰恰成为了围绕林璎作品争议的根源。若干年后，林璎在回忆当时的情形时写道："一开始我就常常想，如果当时我的参赛设计图不是匿名的第1026号，而写明了是由林璎设计的，我会中选吗？"今天，林璎不仅是享誉世界的建筑师，她的个人肖像也挂在了华盛顿特区的国家肖像馆里，越战纪念碑也成为了美国首都最动人心魄的地标之一。

Vocabulary

62.	人类	**rénlèi**	mankind
63.	文明	**wénmíng**	civilization
64.	涌现出	**yǒngxiànchū**	to emerge
65.	杰出	**jiéchū**	outstanding, superior
66.	标志	**biāozhì**	mark
67.	角度	**jiǎodù**	perspective, angle
68.	艺术界	**yìshùjiè**	the arts field
69.	任何	**rènhé**	any
70.	领域	**lǐngyù**	field

71.	技巧	jìqiǎo	technique, craftsmanship
72.	天赋	tiānfù	innate talent, natural gift
73	导师	dǎoshī	advisor, master
74.	知名	zhīmíng	famous
75.	雕塑家	diāosùjiā	sculptor
76.	生涯	shēngyá	career, life
77.	学徒	xuétú	apprentice
78.	媲美	pìměi	to rival, to compare favorably against
79.	绘制	huìzhì	to draw, to design
80.	耶稣	Yēsū	Jesus
81.	受洗	shòuxǐ	to be baptized
82.	手持	shǒuchí	to hold in the hand
83.	衣袍	yīpáo	robe
84.	天使	tiānshǐ	angel
85.	遥远	yáoyuǎn	distant
86.	特区	tèqū	special district (referring to Washington, D.C. in this context)
87.	越战	Yuè Zhàn	Vietnam War
88.	纪念碑	jìniànbēi	memorial, monument
89.	设计者	shèjìzhě	designer
90.	筹建	chóujiàn	to prepare to construct (something)
91.	就…	jiù...	with regard to..., concerning...
92.	举办	jǔbàn	to conduct
93.	竞赛	jìngsài	competition
94.	参赛	cānsài	to participate in a competition
95.	由…组成	yóu...zǔchéng	to be composed of...
96.	评委会	píngwěihuì	appraisal committee, panel of judges
97.	匿名	nìmíng	anonymous
98.	评审	píngshěn	to examine and evaluate
99.	击败	jībài	to defeat, to beat
100.	选手	xuǎnshǒu	contestant
101.	有名气	yǒu míngqi	renowned
102.	惊讶	jīngyà	surprised

103.	中选	**zhòngxuǎn**	to be selected
104.	公布	**gōngbù**	to announce
105.	立即	**lìjí**	immediately
106.	引起	**yǐnqǐ**	to give rise to, to arouse
107.	争议	**zhēngyì**	controversy, dispute
108.	遭到	**zāodào**	to meet with, to encounter
109.	激烈	**jīliè**	intense
110.	讽刺意味	**fěngcì yìwèi**	sarcastic implication, irony
111.	规定	**guīdìng**	to stipulate; a stipulation
112.	政治色彩	**zhèngzhì sècǎi**	political flavor
113.	围绕	**wéirào**	to revolve around
114.	根源	**gēnyuán**	source, root
115.	若干	**ruògān**	a certain number or amount
116.	享誉	**xiǎngyù**	to enjoy fame
117.	建筑师	**jiànzhùshī**	architect
118.	肖像	**xiàoxiàng**	portrait
119.	动人心魄	**dòngrén xīnpò**	to touch one's heart and soul
120.	地标	**dìbiāo**	landmark

Discussion questions (discuss in English or Chinese):

1. Another proverb that can be applied to Leonardo DaVinci and Maya Lin is "youth are to be regarded with awe" (后生可畏 **hòushēng kěwèi**). How does it relate to the proverb in this chapter?*

2. If you are a teacher, have you ever had students who were so smart and motivated that you were sure from early on that they would soon outshine you? And over time, how did these students develop?

3. Another great teacher in Chinese history is Mencius. According to him, one of the three greatest joys in life is getting to teach the outstanding talents in the world. What do you think of this idea in light of the teaching profession in our society today?

---

* This proverb comes from Confucius. The story in Chinese can be found here: https://zhidao.baidu.com/question/559677363.html

Choosing Between Fish and Bear Paws

The great humanist philosopher Mencius believed that it is in mankind's nature to love righteousness even more than life itself. If this is true, then why are men's actions often contrary to their nature? The following narrative will not solve the puzzle, but it does provide more food for thought on the subject.

Mencius said, "I like fish and I also like bear paws. If I cannot have both, then I'll take the bear paws and forego the fish." The notion that "one cannot have both fish and bear paws" has become a proverb that describes the dilemma of having to make a choice between two options. Actually, choosing between fish and bear paws should not have been difficult, because either way Mencius would get something he enjoyed. If he had chosen the fish instead, he would have been equally happy. But right after this light-hearted opening, Mencius turned the dilemma of having to make a choice into something deadly serious.

Mencius continued, "Life is something I crave, and righteousness too. But if I cannot have both, then I will choose righteousness over life. While I crave life, there is something I crave even more than life; therefore I would not sacrifice the thing of greater value only to hold on to life. Death is something that I abhor, but there is something I abhor even more than death. Therefore, there are certain perils that I will not avoid in order to avoid death. But if people crave life more than anything else in the world, then is there anything they will not do to stay alive? And if people abhor death more than anything else in the world, then is there anything they will not do to avoid death? In truth, there are certain evils we will not commit in order to stay alive or to avoid death. From this, we can see that there are certain things we crave more than life and certain things that we abhor more than death. It's not only the virtuous among

鱼与熊掌，不可兼得

孟子是中国古代一位伟大的思想家。他崇尚人道主义，并认为人的本性是把道义看得比生命更重要。如果人的本性真是这样的话，那为什么人们的行为常常与他们的本性恰恰相反呢？下面的这篇短文虽然并不能为我们解开这个谜，但至少可以给我们一些启示。

孟子说："我喜欢吃鱼，也喜欢吃熊掌。如果我不能两样都得到的话，那我就会放弃鱼而选择吃熊掌。"如今"鱼与熊掌不可兼得"已经成为了一个谚语，用来描述一个人必须在两者当中选择其一的困惑。实际上，选择鱼还是熊掌并不是一个难题，因为不管选择哪一个，孟子都会喜欢。如果他最终选择了鱼，也会一样地开心。不过，在这句轻松的开场白之后，孟子话锋一转，将两者必选其一的困惑变成了一个生死攸关的严肃话题。

孟子继续说道："生是我渴求的，义也是我渴求的。假如只能选择一个，那我会舍生而取义。虽然我渴求生，但还有比生更重要的事情，因此我不会选择苟且偷生。我厌恶死，但还有比死更让我厌恶的事情。因此，有些险恶的事情我不会为了保全性命而逃避。如果人们把生命看得比世界上其他任何事情都更重要的话，就会想尽一切办法来保全性命吧？假如人们在这个世上最厌恶的事情就是死亡，那么凡是可以让他们逃避死亡的事情，他们还有什么不会去做的呢？事实上，人们都不会为了保全性命或者逃避死亡而情愿做一些邪恶的事情。由此可见，人们所渴求的还有比生命更重要的东西，人们所厌恶的也还有比死亡更可怕的事

us who have this mentality; we all have it. The only difference is that the virtuous among us can prevent the loss of this mentality.

"To those who are dying of hunger, a bowl of food or a ladle of soup can mean the difference between life and death. And yet if you call to them disdainfully, they would rather die than accept the food. If you kick the food over to a beggar, he would not stoop to look at it.

"But nowadays there are those who would accept a high salary from a ruler regardless of the ruler's impropriety. If it were me, I would want to ask, 'What would that high salary get me? A beautiful mansion? The services of wives and concubines? Or the ability to help my poor and needy associates?' Recalling how those dying of famine would rather die than accept food disdainfully tossed to them, I wonder how those officials could accept high salaries from unrighteous rulers in order to have the services of wives and concubines or to assist their own needy associates? Why can't they be like the beggars and decline those offers? This is what is meant by 'losing mankind's innate nature.'"

情。这种理念不只是<u>圣贤</u>才有，我们每个人都有，而<u>唯一</u>不同的是圣贤不会<u>丢弃</u>这种理念。

　　"对快要饿死的人来说，得到一<u>筐</u>饭和一碗汤就可以<u>活命</u>，得不到就会饿死。然而，要是你不客气地<u>吆喝</u>他们，他们<u>宁可饿死</u>也不要接受这样的<u>嗟来之食</u>。假如你用脚把食物<u>踢</u>给一个<u>乞丐</u>，他也<u>不屑于弯下腰</u>去看一眼这样的食物。

　　"如今，有些人不管<u>君王</u>的做法是不是<u>合乎礼仪</u>就接受高薪俸禄。如果是我的话，就会<u>扪心自问</u>'这样的高薪俸禄会给我带来什么呢？<u>华丽</u>的<u>住宅</u>？<u>妻妾的侍奉</u>？或是我可以因此<u>救助</u>那些<u>贫穷</u>并需要帮助的<u>门生</u>呢？'想想那些快要饿死的人宁可死也不接受嗟来之食，我真不明白那些<u>为官之人</u>怎么能够接受<u>不义</u>君王的高薪俸禄，<u>从而</u>享受妻妾的侍奉，救助需要他们帮助的门生？为什么他们不能像乞丐一样<u>拒绝</u>嗟来之食呢？在我看来，这就是<u>失去</u>人之本性了。"

Mencius was not just an armchair philosopher. The above narrative was based on his personal experience. Being an itinerant teacher during the Warring States period, it was his dream to find a ruler who would listen to his humanistic teachings and put them into practice, perhaps even ushering in a new peaceful dynasty. After traveling for many years and having many audiences with various rulers, Mencius finally secured a high position in the state of Qi. For a while it seemed that his long-cherished dream might be realized. But soon the King of Qi waged war against a neighboring state, and it became clear to Mencius that the king had used him to mask his own aggression. In despair, Mencius realized that he could never be the philosopher standing behind a good ruler, so he voluntarily ended his career as a political advisor.

The Chinese proverb

鱼	与	熊	掌,	不	可	兼	得
yú	yǔ	xióng	zhǎng,	bù	kě	jiān	dé
fish	and	bear	paws,	not	can	both	to get

Literal meaning: One cannot have both fish and bear paws; one must choose one or the other.

Connotation:

1) Positive interpretation: You are in the fortunate position of having two good options (like the two delicacies of fish and bear paws), even if you cannot have both. The implication is that you cannot go wrong with either one and therefore should be content with either.

2) Somewhat negative interpretation: You are having to weigh the pros and cons of two options and decide which one to choose. The implication is that whichever choice you make, you have to accept compromises.

The original source: "Gaozi, Part I," a chapter in the *Book of Mencius*. Mencius lived in 372–289 BCE. The book bearing his name was most likely assembled by his disciples ca. 300 BCE.《孟子 • 告子上》（约公元前300年由孟子弟子们编辑）。孟子在世于公元前372–289年。

孟子并不是一位空谈的思想家。上面的这篇短文是根据他的亲身经历而写成的。作为战国时期周游列国的老师，孟子渴望找到一位君王，接受自己的仁政主张，甚至于开创一个太平盛世的王朝。孟子周游列国多年，游说过多位君王以后，终于在齐国得到了一个相当高的职位。当时孟子感觉自己长久以来的梦想似乎就要实现了。但没过多久，齐王就对邻国发动了战争，这样一来，孟子看清了齐王原来只是利用他的主张来伪装自己的野心，随即就意识到自己这一生不可能实现辅佐一位明君的梦想了。失望之余，孟子主动结束了自己的从政生涯。

Vocabulary

1.	兼得	**jiāndé**	to attain both
2.	崇尚	**chóngshàng**	to advocate, to uphold
3.	人道主义	**réndào zhǔyì**	humanism
4.	本性	**běnxìng**	innate nature
5.	道义	**dàoyì**	righteousness
6.	行为	**xíngwéi**	actions, behavior
7.	恰恰相反	**qiàqià xiāngfǎn**	exactly the opposite
8.	解开…谜	**jiěkāi...mí**	to solve a puzzle
9.	启示	**qǐshì**	inspiration, enlightenment
10.	熊掌	**xióngzhǎng**	bear paws
11.	放弃	**fàngqì**	to relinquish, to give up
12.	谚语	**yànyǔ**	proverb, saying
13.	描述	**miáoshù**	to depict
14.	两者当中 选择其一	**liǎngzhě dāngzhōng xuǎnzé qíyī**	to choose one from two options
15.	困惑	**kùnhuò**	perplexity, dilemma

16.	难题	nántí	difficult problem
17.	开场白	kāichǎngbái	opening remarks, prologue
18.	话锋一转	huàfēng yìzhuǎn	to abruptly turn the focus of the discussion
19.	生死攸关	shēngsǐ yōuguān	a vital matter
20.	严肃	yánsù	serious, somber
21.	渴求	kěqiú	to thirst for, to earnestly seek
22.	舍生而取义	shěshēng ér qǔyì	to die for the sake of a just cause
23.	苟且偷生	gǒuqiě tōushēng	to drag out a shameful existence
24.	厌恶	yànwù	to detest
25.	险恶	xiǎn'è	peril (note the difference in pronunciation of 恶, depending on whether it means the verb "to detest" or the noun "evil")
26.	保全	bǎoquán	to preserve
27.	性命	xìngmìng	life
28.	逃避	táobì	to avoid, to evade
29.	任何	rènhé	any, whatever
30.	死亡	sǐwáng	death
31.	凡是	fánshì	every, any, whatever
32.	情愿	qíngyuàn	would rather ... (than ...)
33.	邪恶	xié'è	evil, wickedness
34.	由此可见	yóu cǐ kě jiàn	it can be seen from this
35.	理念	lǐniàn	concept, belief
36.	圣贤	shèngxián	sage (noun)
37.	唯一	wéiyī	only, solely
38.	丢弃	diūqì	to lose, to relinquish
39.	筐	kuāng	basket
40.	活命	huómìng	to survive, to save one's life
41.	吆喝	yāohe	to loudly or rudely call out
42.	宁可	nìngkě	would rather ...
43.	嗟来之食	jiēlái zhī shí	food rudely offered

44.	踢	tī	to kick
45.	乞丐	qǐgài	beggars
46.	不屑于	búxièyú	will not deign to ...
47.	弯下腰	wānxià yāo	to stoop
48.	君王	jūnwáng	ruler, king
49.	合乎礼仪	héhū lǐyí	to accord with proper etiquette
50.	高薪俸禄	gāoxīn fènglù	high salary of an official
51.	扪心自问	ménxīn zìwèn	to ask oneself in good conscience
52.	华丽	huálì	luxurious
53.	住宅	zhùzhái	residence
54.	妻妾	qīqiè	wives and concubines
55.	侍奉	shìfèng	to wait upon; deferential service
56.	救助	qiúzhù	to seek help
57.	贫穷	pínqióng	poor, needy
58.	门生	ménshēng	followers
59.	为官之人	wéi guān zhī rén	those who are officials
60.	不义	búyì	unrighteous
61.	从而	cóng'ér	thus, thereby
62.	拒绝	jùjué	to refuse, to reject
63.	失去	shīqù	to lose
64.	空谈	kōngtán	empty talk
65.	亲身经历	qīnshēn jīnglì	personal experience
66.	周游列国	zhōuyóu lièguó	to travel through various countries
67.	仁政	rénzhèng	humane governance
68.	主张	zhǔzhāng	to advocate; viewpoint, proposition
69.	开创	kāichuàng	to initiate
70.	太平盛世	tàipíng shèngshì	a peaceful and prosperous world
71.	游说	yóushuì	to travel around and persuade
72.	职位	zhíwèi	official position
73.	发动	fādòng	to launch

74. 利用	lìyòng	to take advantage of
75. 伪装	wěizhuāng	to feign, to mask
76. 野心	yěxīn	ambition
77. 随即	suíjí	soon thereafter

....

The Proverb in Modern Usage

Juggling Career and Family Life

Mencius used the proverb "one cannot have both fish and bear paws" as a metaphor for ethical dilemmas which warrant agonizing soul-searching. However the modern usage of this proverb is more light-hearted and is usually applied to making a choice between two equally good options. Nothing is perfect, and even good options have pros and cons.

My former student Jennifer, who recently completed her Ph.D., has been a part-time lecturer at a university, and is now poised to apply for a full-time position. She and her husband Daniel of eight years have methodically planned their future together. So imagine their surprise when they found out that they were expecting their first child! Since Jennifer sees me as a role model who has successfully juggled an academic career while raising two kids, she came to me for advice. Having spent the last ten years getting her Ph.D., she is eager to get on with her career, especially since good jobs in academia are becoming more and more competitive. But she and Daniel also feel strongly that their child in the first year of life should be cared for by the parents themselves. Jennifer is consid-

78.	意识到	**yìshi dào**	to realize
79.	辅佐	**fǔzuǒ**	to assist (a ruler)
80.	明君	**míngjūn**	enlightened ruler
81.	从政生涯	**cóngzhèng shēngyá**	political career

事业与家庭能否兼得？

孟子用"鱼与熊掌不可兼得"来比喻人们在伦理道义方面的困惑，这自然会引发人们在灵魂深处进行一番苦苦思索。然而，这个谚语在今天运用起来却是轻松得多，并大多是在两个好的选项中做出选择。世间本无完美的事情，最好的选项也会有利有弊。

　　珍妮是我以前的一个学生，目前在一所大学兼课。最近她刚取得了博士学位，就打算找一个正式的教职。她与结婚八年的丈夫丹诺一直把两人的生活规划得有条有理。这时，珍妮突然发现自己怀孕了，可想而知他们是多么地惊讶！珍妮一向都认为我既在事业上很有成就又带大了一双很有出息的儿女，所以总把我看作她的楷模，于是来找我咨询。珍妮花了十年的时间才取得博士学位，而且现在谋求好教职的竞争越来越激烈，所以她很想先追求一番事业。可是她和丈夫又都确信孩子一岁以前应该由父母亲自来照顾。

ering taking a gap year to be a full-time mother, but she is worried that prospective employers down the road will see her as a candidate who prioritizes family life above professional commitments. As she thinks about forging ahead with a full-time position now, she worries about the possible lifelong repercussions on her child. Having lived through that dilemma myself a generation ago, I understand Jennifer's predicament, but I still don't have the right answer for her. When I was at that crossroads, I chose to forge ahead with my career. But I will never know if things might have turned out better or worse had I chosen to take a gap year. What I ended up telling Jennifer was that she and Daniel are fortunate to have two promising careers and to soon be parents to a long-awaited child. Then I proceeded to help them think about the ways in which the negative aspects of each option could be mitigated. Soon they realized that there is no clear right or wrong choice, but what is more important is how they manage the pros and cons that come with their choice. Given Jennifer and Daniel's resourcefulness, I am confident that they will succeed in their careers and in raising their family. Still, I am anxiously awaiting the arrival of their baby and hope that Jennifer will soon resolve her "fish and bear paws" dilemma.

于是，珍妮考虑休一年的<u>产假</u>，在家里做全职母亲，可是她又担心将来找工作的时候，<u>雇主</u>会认为她是一个<u>优先考虑</u>家庭而将事业放在第二位的人。要是她现在全身心追求事业呢，又担心会给孩子留下永久的<u>创伤</u>。作为老一辈的<u>过来人</u>，我完全理解珍妮的困惑，可是也想不出一个很好的<u>解困</u>办法。我自己从前<u>身处</u>那个十字路口的时候，选择了<u>全力以赴</u>地追求事业。现在回头去看，我真的不知道如果当时选择了休假一年的话，结果会更好还是更糟。我最终告诉珍妮，她跟丹诺两个人的事业<u>前景</u>很好，而且<u>期盼</u>已久的孩子又很快要<u>降生</u>，实在是非常幸福。接着我又帮他们设想如何减轻两种选项中不同的<u>负面影响</u>。他们夫妻两人很快就意识到摆在面前的两种选择并没有明显的<u>对错之分</u>，而更重要的是在他们做出选择之后，如何<u>管控</u>好<u>随之而来</u>的利弊。珍妮和丹诺都很能干，所以我相信他们既可以在事业上成功，也能同时照顾好孩子。我<u>期待</u>着他们宝宝降生的好消息，也希望珍妮能早日在"鱼与熊掌"之间做出<u>抉择</u>。

Vocabulary

82.	能否	**néngfǒu**	can or cannot
83.	比喻	**bǐyù**	to serve as an analogy, to draw a parallel
84.	伦理	**lúnlǐ**	moral principles
85.	灵魂深处	**línghún shēnchù**	the depth of one's soul
86.	苦苦思索	**kǔkǔ sīsuǒ**	to think hard and deeply
87.	运用	**yùnyòng**	to apply
88.	选项	**xuǎnxiàng**	options, choices
89.	有利有弊	**yǒulì yǒubì**	to have pluses and minuses
90.	兼课	**jiānkè**	to teach part-time
91.	教职	**jiàozhí**	teaching position
92.	规划	**guīhuà**	to plan, to map out
93.	有条有理	**yǒutiáo yǒulǐ**	systematic, orderly
94.	怀孕	**huáiyùn**	to be pregnant
95.	惊讶	**jīngyà**	to be surprised
96.	既…又…	**jì...yòu...**	to be both ... and ...
97.	有出息	**yǒu chūxi**	to have good potential, destined to go far
98.	楷模	**kǎimó**	role model
99.	咨询	**zīxún**	to consult with, to seek information from
100.	谋求	**móuqiú**	to seek
101.	激烈	**jīliè**	intense
102.	追求	**zhuīqiú**	to pursue
103.	产假	**chǎnjià**	maternity leave
104.	雇主	**gùzhǔ**	employer
105.	优先	**yōuxiān**	priority
106.	创伤	**chuāngshāng**	wound, trauma
107.	过来人	**guòláirén**	someone who has been through it all
108.	解困	**jiěkùn**	to resolve a dilemma
109.	身处	**shēnchǔ**	to be in a particular circumstance
110.	全力以赴	**quánlì yǐ fù**	to go all out

111.	前景	qiánjǐng	future prospects
112.	期盼	qīpàn	to look forward to, to await (stronger than 期待 below)
113.	降生	jiàngshēng	to be born
114.	负面影响	fùmiàn yǐngxiǎng	negative effects
115.	对错之分	duìcuò zhī fēn	difference between right and wrong
116.	管控	guǎnkòng	to manage and control
117.	随之而来	suí zhī ér lái	to come along with
118.	期待	qīdài	to look forward to
119.	抉择	juézé	decision, resolution

Discussion questions (discuss in English or Chinese):

1. Have you ever been in the enviable position of having two job offers that seemed in balance to be equally good? If so, how did you make your choice and what was the outcome?

2. Is there a proverb from your native language that is similar to the Chinese proverb "you cannot have both fish and bear paws"?

3. Can you think of examples to substantiate Mencius' claim that it is in mankind's nature to choose righteousness over life? What about the opposite? Given both kinds of examples, would you agree with Mencius that human nature is innately good?

An Imposter in the Orchestra

Around 300 BCE, the State of Qi was ruled by King Xuan. This king was tyrannical, and loved grandiose displays made on his behalf. He enjoyed listening to music played on the *yu* (a kind of reed pipe) but he had the imperious quirk of demanding that a throng of 300 musicians play for him at the same time. The finest reed pipers from far and wide gathered at his court and were treated royally by the king. There was a crafty ne'er-do-well called Nanguo who saw this as a great opportunity to wheedle his way into the huge *yu* ensemble. Nanguo had never touched a *yu* in his life, but he was a slick talker and somehow managed to sweet talk the King into believing that he was a fabulous *yu* player. Nanguo was also an expert imitator—his movements, body language and facial expressions looked exactly like those of a real musician. So for a good number of years, Nanguo received the same royal treatment as all the other 299 musicians. None of his colleagues dared expose him because the King had personally welcomed him into the orchestra. Nanguo thought he had it made! Well, there may be an occasional free lunch, but it doesn't last forever.

Eventually King Xuan died and was succeeded by his son King Min. King Min also enjoyed *yu* music. Moreover he was an aficionado who *really* knew how to enjoy this kind of music—by listening to each musician individually. The new king decreed that henceforth each of the 300 *yu* players would take turns playing solo for his discerning ear. When Nanguo heard this news, he was in the middle of enjoying one of his lavish meals. In shock, he dropped his bowl and chopsticks right on the floor. He knew his number was up! Getting kicked out of the orchestra was the least of his problems; he might even be executed for deceiving the king! In a flash, he disappeared into the night without even taking his *yu* or any of his belongings. He was never heard from again, and King Min never missed having one less musician in his orchestra.

滥竽充数

大约公元前300年，齐宣王统治着齐国。齐宣王不但是一个暴君，还特别爱讲排场。他喜欢听吹竽，而且每次都要三百名乐手一起演奏给他一个人听，以显示国君的威严。远近闻名的吹竽高手都集中到了齐宣王的宫廷里，享受着国君给他们的优厚待遇。一个名叫南郭先生的混混儿，觉得这是一个混入吹竽大乐队的好机会。南郭先生以前根本没有摸过竽，不过他是个能说会道的吹牛大王，成功地让齐宣王相信他是难得的吹竽高手。南郭先生很会装腔作势，演奏的时候身体摇来摆去，十分动情忘我的样子，看上去就像一名吹竽高手。在后来好几年的时间里，南郭先生享受着其他299位乐手一样的优厚待遇，而且正因为他是齐宣王亲自带进乐队里的人，也没有人敢站出来揭发他。南郭先生以为他可以这样混下去了，因此暗地里沾沾自喜，很是得意。不过呀，这世界上可能有免费的午餐，但是一定不会让一个混混儿吃一辈子！

　　齐宣王死了以后，他的儿子齐湣王继承了王位。湣王也喜欢听吹竽，而且真正懂得欣赏音乐，因此他每次只让一位乐手独奏。湣王下令300名乐手一个一个地为他演奏吹竽。南郭先生听到这个坏消息的时候，正在享用一顿丰盛的大餐，于是吓得碗和筷子都掉到了地上。他当然没法子在乐队里混下去了，不过被踢出乐队是小事儿，更糟的是，他很可能会因为欺骗了国君而被杀头呢！这时，南郭先生连自己的竽和家什都顾不上收拾，就连夜逃之夭夭了。后来，谁也没有再听到他的消息，湣王当然也不在乎宫廷里少了一名冒牌的乐手。

The author of this story is the great legalist philosopher and political theoretician Han Feizi (280–233 BCE). One theme that he emphasized in his writings on "how to be a good ruler" was the importance of employing capable and righteous advisors. In conveying his message that a ruler must evaluate candidates carefully and scrutinize each one individually, Han Feizi avoided using contemporary examples that might have been too sensitive. He chose instead the historical example of a phony musician who lived far enough in the past to have been forgotten, and he also added a dose of humor to sweeten an otherwise stern message.

这个故事的作者是战国时期著名的思想家及法家学派的代表人物韩非子（公元前280–233年）。韩非子写过许多论述"如何成为一位明君"的文章，其中强调的一个主题就是君王任用正直能干的人才以辅佐朝政的重要性。韩非子要告诫当时的君王必须精心慎选人才，但他不能触及比较敏感的当代事例，所以选用了历史上那位滥竽充数的乐手作为例子，一来时过境迁不再那么敏感，二来这个幽默的故事也给一个本来很严肃的话题增添了一点趣味性。

The Chinese Proverb

滥	竽	充	数
làn	yú	chōng	shù
unscrupulous	reed instrument	to fill in	number

Literal meaning: An unscrupulous *yu* player filling in the ranks

Connotations:

1. An unqualified person who disguises himself by mixing in with those who are truly qualified

2. An inferior person or thing included to fill in the requisite number

3. A self-effacing way to say that one is not as good as his/her peers in a given group

The original source: "Internal Collected Discourse, Part I," in *Han Feizi*. Warring States period, 3rd century BCE. 《韩非子•内储说上》（战国时期公元前第三世纪）

Vocabulary

1.	统治	**tǒngzhì**	to govern, to rule over
2.	暴君	**bàojūn**	tyrannical ruler
3.	讲排场	**jiǎng páichang**	fond of being ostentatious
4.	吹竽	**chuīyú**	to play the wind instrument *yu* (a kind of reed)
5.	乐手	**yuèshǒu**	skilled musician
6.	演奏	**yǎnzòu**	to perform
7.	国君	**guójūn**	king of a feudal state
8.	威严	**wēiyán**	prestige, dignity
9.	远近闻名	**yuǎnjìn wénmíng**	renowned near and far
10.	高手	**gāoshǒu**	an expert (at doing something)
11.	集中	**jízhōng**	congregated, centralized, concentrated
12.	宫廷	**gōngtíng**	palace, court
13.	享受	**xiǎngshòu**	to enjoy, to receive/enjoy certain benefits
14.	优厚待遇	**yōuhòu dàiyù**	generous treatment/remuneration
15.	混混儿	**hùnhùnr**	rascal, bum
16.	混入	**hùnrù**	to slip into (furtively)
17.	乐队	**yuèduì**	orchestra
18.	能说会道	**néngshuō huìdào**	to be a good talker
19.	吹牛大王	**chuīniú dàwáng**	"king of boasting"
20.	难得	**nándé**	hard to come by, rare
21.	装腔作势	**zhuāngqiāng zuòshì**	to strike a pose, to be pretentious
22.	摇来摆去	**yáolái bǎiqù**	to sway back and forth
23.	动情忘我	**dòngqíng wàngwǒ**	to be obliviously enraptured
24.	亲自	**qīnzì**	personally; … himself
25.	揭发	**jiēfā**	to expose
26.	暗地里	**àndìli**	secretly
27.	沾沾自喜	**zhānzhān zìxǐ**	pleased with oneself
28.	得意	**déyì**	proud of oneself, complacent
29.	免费	**miǎnfèi**	free
30.	一辈子	**yíbèizi**	one's whole life, a lifetime
31.	继承	**jìchéng**	to follow (in a position), to succeed

32. 王位	wángwèi	throne
33. 欣赏	xīnshǎng	to appreciate
34. 独奏	dúzòu	solo performance
35. 下令	xiàlìng	to issue an order
36. 丰盛	fēngshèng	lavish
37. 于是	yúshì	thereupon, therefore
38. 吓	xià	to frighten; frightened
39. 踢出	tīchū	to be kicked out
40. 更糟的是	gèng zāode shì	what's worse
41. 欺骗	qīpiàn	to deceive
42. 杀头	shātóu	to be decapitated
43. 家什	jiāshi	household stuff (colloquial)
44. 顾不上	gùbushàng	unable to attend to
45. 连夜	liányè	that very night
46. 逃之夭夭	táo zhī yāoyāo	to have escaped and was nowhere to be found
47. 不在乎	búzàihu	not care about
48. 冒牌	màopái	fake
49. 著名	zhùmíng	famous
50. 法家学派	fǎjiā xuépài	Legalist school of thought
51. 人物	rénwù	personage, notable person
52. 论述	lùnshù	to expound
53. 明君	míngjūn	enlightened ruler
54. 强调	qiángdiào	to emphasize
55. 主题	zhǔtí	topic
56. 任用	rènyòng	to employ, to appoint to a position
57. 正直	zhèngzhí	upstanding, virtuous
58. 辅佐	fǔzuǒ	to assist (a ruler in governance)
59. 朝政	cháozhèng	court administration, governance of a country
60. 告诫	gàojiè	to admonish
61. 精心	jīngxīn	meticulous
62. 慎选	shènxuǎn	to select carefully
63. 触及	chùjí	to touch on

64. 敏感	mǐn'gǎn	sensitive
65. 事例	shìlì	instance, case
66. 一来⋯二来⋯	yìlái...èrlái...	for one thing ..., for another ...
67. 时过境迁	shíguò jìngqiān	the time has passed and the circumstances have changed

A College Admissions Scandal

It is common practice among elite institutions in the U.S. to give preferential treatment to applicants who are the offspring of alumni, faculty or donors. This practice disrupts the level playing field and is therefore controversial. But crossing the line from unfair to fraudulent is beyond controversial. In 2019, a college admissions bribery scam came to light at eleven elite American universities and their associated athletic programs. The chief culprit was charged with organizing and selling fraudulent college admissions services and he pleaded guilty. The thirty-three parents involved in the case—clients of the culprit—were all rich and famous. Some claimed that they were duped into thinking that their donations were welcomed by the institutions and totally legitimate. The most unfortunate victims were the students admitted through this fraudulent scheme. They themselves may not have instigated the deceit but they were unwitting parties—and ultimately victims—to it. Even though they might have been academically qualified to attend the institutions to which they were admitted, they could be scorned as "imposters in the ranks."

68.	幽默	**yōumò**	humorous, humor
69.	严肃	**yánsù**	serious, solemn
70.	增添	**zēngtiān**	to add
71.	趣味性	**qùwèixìng**	interest

....

大学招生骗局

美国精英大学在录取新生的时候，通常会给予校友、教师以及捐款人的子女优先考虑。对于这种做法，人们褒贬不一，因为专门为一部分人破例不符合公平竞争的原则。但是从不符合公平原则越界到徇私舞弊是绝对不行的。2019年，一起美国大学招生贿赂丑闻由媒体曝光。目前，这个案件仍在调查中，也许还要经过许多年才能结案。十一所精英大学以及所属的某些运动队卷入了其中。这起舞弊案件的主犯被控以造假的手段为客户提供高校录取服务，并从中牟利，而他本人也已经认罪。涉及这起案件的33个家庭——即被控罪犯的客户们——都来自名门或是富裕家庭。有些家庭声称他们误以为自己的捐款是受到学校欢迎的，也是完全合法的。在这起诈骗案中，最不幸的受害者就是那些被高校录取的学生。他们本人也许并没有主动地参与这起诈骗案，但却在不知情的情况下受到了牵连，而最终成为了受害者。尽管这些学生在学业上有可能已经达到了录取院校的标准，但他们很可能会被视为"混入精英乐队中的冒牌货"。

Vocabulary

72.	招生	zhāoshēng	to recruit students
73.	骗局	piànjú	hoax, fraud
74.	精英	jīngyīng	elite
75.	录取	lùqǔ	to admit (students)
76.	给予	jǐyǔ	to render, to give (formal)
77.	校友	xiàoyǒu	alumni
78.	捐款	juānkuǎn	to donate money
79.	优先	yōuxiān	favorable, priority
80.	褒贬不一	bāobiǎn bùyī	to differ in praise and disparagement
81.	破例	pòlì	exception
82.	符合	fúhé	to accord with
83.	原则	yuánzé	principle
84.	越界	yuèjiè	to cross the line
85.	徇私	xùnsī	to practice favoritism; nepotism
86.	舞弊	wǔbì	fraudulent practice
87.	起	qǐ	a measure word applied to incidents (accidents or crimes)
88.	贿赂	huìlù	bribery
89.	丑闻	chǒuwén	scandal
90.	媒体	méitǐ	media
91.	曝光	bàoguāng	to expose, to reveal (a secret)
92.	案件	ànjiàn	case (crime, lawsuit, etc.)
93.	调查	diàochá	to investigate
94.	结案	jié'àn	to conclude a legal case
95.	所属的	suǒshǔde	subsidiary
96.	卷入	juǎnrù	to be drawn into, to be involved in
97.	主犯	zhǔfàn	prime culprit
98.	被控	bèikòng	the accused
99.	造假	zàojiǎ	to fabricate (falsehood)
100.	手段	shǒuduàn	tactics
101.	客户	kèhù	clients
102.	从中牟利	cóngzhōng móulì	to profit illicitly from the act
103.	认罪	rènzuì	to admit guilt, to plead guilty
104.	涉及	shèjí	to involve

105.	即	jí	that is, i.e.
106.	罪犯	zuìfàn	culprit, criminal
107.	名门	míngmén	eminent families
108.	富裕	fùyù	wealthy
109.	声称	shēngchēng	to profess, to claim
110.	误以为	wùyǐwéi	to mistakenly think
111.	合法	héfǎ	legal
112.	诈骗	zhàpiàn	to swindle, to defraud
113.	受害者	shòuhàizhě	victim
114.	高校	gāoxiào	institutions of higher learning
115.	主动地	zhǔdòngde	take initiative (in doing something)
116.	参与	cānyù	to participate in
117.	不知情	bù zhīqíng	to be ignorant about something; un-knowingly
118.	牵连	qiānlián	to be implicated
119.	学业	xuéyè	academics
120.	标准	biāozhǔn	standards
121.	被视为	bèi shìwéi	to be seen as
122.	冒牌货	màopáihuò	"fake goods," imposter, a phony

Discussion questions (discuss in English or Chinese):

1. Does the phenomenon of "imposters in the orchestra" exist in your culture? Where have you seen it?

2. A group of friends need one more participant for an activity, like a volleyball game, so they invite you. If you are not enthusiastic about joining, would you beg off by saying something like, "I'd only be an imposter among the true players; you're better off finding someone else to fill the slot"? (A Chinese person may use this as a modest excuse, but would a Westerner do the same?)

3. As a financial expediency, many colleges and universities in the U.S. are admitting a large number of students from China, even with the knowledge that some of these students are not sufficiently prepared to survive. What can the parents of Chinese students do to make sure their children do not become "imposters in the orchestra"?

People Cannot Be Judged by Their Appearance; Oceans Cannot Be Measured with a Bucket

In bygone days, certain cultures in the world accorded high esteem to courtesans, who were genteel escorts trained in the classical cultural arts. In the early years of the Southern Song dynasty (ca. 1130), in the capital of Lin'an (present-day Hangzhou), there lived a most celebrated courtesan by the name of Huakui ("Preeminent Flower"). Courtesans were all beautiful, but Huakui was exceptional in that she was refined and well-educated. Not only was she skilled in the feminine arts like needlework and embroidery, she could match any man in calligraphy, painting, chess, music or poetry. In reality, she had been lovingly raised as the only child in a good family in the Northern Song capital of Kaifeng, which was destroyed by the Jurchens when they attacked China. The Jurchens established their own dynasty in the North, forcing the Song dynasty to retreat to the South. When Huakui's family fled the Jurchens, Huakui—who was twelve at the time—became separated from her parents in the chaos and was eventually sold to a brothel in the new Song capital.

Huakui soon became the most coveted courtesan in Lin'an. Even though her madam charged clients the exorbitant sum of ten ounces of silver for a night with her, she always had a waiting list extending over a month. Her clients were the wealthiest and most powerful gentlemen of all ages, but that didn't stop other men who could never dream of touching her from desiring her. Indeed, a young oil peddler by the name of Zhu Zhong became so enamored of her that he made it his life's goal to spend one night with her. He doubled his work hours and saved every penny. Whenever he accumulated enough coins to convert them into an ounce of silver, he would sheepishly take them to the silver shop to trade. The silver smith was so touched by Zhu Zhong's determination that he put aside his initial disdain for this foolish oil peddler and thought to himself: a man cannot be gauged by his appearance, just as the water in

人不可貌相，
海水不可斗量

很久以前，世界上一些国家的文化很尊崇名妓。在人们眼里，这些名妓都是受过古典文化艺术熏陶的高雅伴侣。在南宋初年（大约公元1130年），京城临安府住着一位名叫花魁的名妓。一般来说，名妓都十分漂亮，而花魁更加出色，因为她是个优雅的才女。花魁不但擅长女红刺绣，而且吟诗作赋，琴棋书画，都比得过男子。花魁本来是北宋京城开封府一户好人家里受宠爱的独生女，女真族攻打宋朝，毁了开封，并在北方建立起自己的政权后，宋朝政权不得不搬迁到了南方，而住在开封府的很多百姓也只好逃往南方。在逃难的混乱中，当时才12岁的花魁和父母走散了，最终在宋朝新的京城被卖到烟花巷里，成了一名青楼女子。

花魁很快就成为了临安府里最红的名妓。鸨娘利用她来收取的费用特别高，一夜要十两白银，但慕名前来的男人还是排起了长龙，常常要等一个多月。花魁的嫖客多半是城里有钱有势的人，老老少少都有。然而，那些没钱没势的穷小子也并非没动过一样的念头。比方说，附近有个叫朱重的卖油郎也为花魁的美貌倾倒，一心只想跟花魁度过一个美好的夜晚，不然死也不会甘心。于是朱重每天加倍干活儿，并且省下每一个铜板。每当他攒够了铜板，就怯生生地拿到银铺去兑换成一两银子。银铺的伙计开始的时候很看不起这个又笨又穷的卖油郎，后来也被他的执着感动了，就心

the ocean cannot be measured with a dipper. It took three years for Zhu Zhong to save up ten ounces of silver. But when he went to the brothel to claim his prize, the madam brushed him off by telling him to clean up his appearance and come back dressed as a gentleman befitting the company of Huakui. Moreover, he would have to wait a couple of months, and his stayover would be at the end of one of Huakui's evenings with her usual clientele.

Zhu Zhong's long-awaited evening finally came. He waited and waited, but then when Huakui arrived, she was staggering and woozy. Zhu Zhong was sad to see her in such a state, but he did what came naturally to him, which was to gently tuck her into bed and sit quietly by her side all night long. When Huakui woke up feeling better the next morning, Zhu Zhong felt that his long-cherished wish had been fulfilled. He then bid her goodbye and went home to catch up on his sleep.

里想：人不可貌相，海水不可斗量。朱重用了三年的时间，终于攒够了十两银子。当朱重带着银子，高高兴兴地到青楼找花魁的时候，鸨娘却再三推托，让朱重把自己好好打扮一下，穿得体面一些，像个绅士一样才配得上花魁。此外，鸨娘告诉朱重得等几个月，而且他跟花魁在一起的那个晚上得等她接待完常客以后才行。

朱重期待的夜晚终于到了。他等了老半天花魁才回来，并且她喝醉了。本性善良的朱重一看见花魁醉得像烂泥一样就为她感到很难过，然后就很自然地把她扶上了床，给她盖好被子，整晚都坐在床边服侍着她。第二天早上花魁醒过来的时候，感觉好多了，朱重就觉得他长久期待的愿望已经实现了。他告别了花魁，便回家补觉去了。

The next encounter between Zhu Zhong and Huakui came a year later. One day while out peddling oil near West Lake, he heard a disheveled lady sobbing by the side of the road. To his shock, it was Huakui! As it turned out, she had been dumped there by a would-be client who was offended because she rejected his advances. Zhu Zhong again did what came naturally, which was to call a sedan chair for her and escort her home on foot himself. When they arrived at the brothel, Huakui revealed her secret to Zhu Zhong: she had been saving all her earnings while waiting to discover her true love, whereupon she would redeem her freedom with her savings. So from that day on, Zhu Zhong and Huakui lived happily ever after.

As you can imagine, all the gentlemen in town dropped their jaws as they marveled at how the lowly oil peddler won Huakui all to himself. Well, the saying "never judge a man by his appearance" is really true. As it turned out, Zhu Zhong also came from a good family in Kaifeng. His family was similarly devastated when Northern Song fell to the Jurchens and he was adopted by a childless oil seller at age thirteen. Before this revelation, everyone saw Zhu Zhong as too lowly a match for Huakui, but in the end they realized that their family backgrounds made them well-suited for each other after all.

朱重再见到花魁是一年以后了。有一天，朱重在西湖边卖油，听到路边一个头发凌乱的妇人哭泣的声音。定睛一看，朱重惊呆了，是花魁！原来，一个嫖客因为花魁拒绝他的非礼而感觉被冒犯了，于是将花魁甩在了路边。朱重又一次表现出他的善良，他叫来了轿夫，让花魁坐在轿子里，自己一路走着护送花魁回家。到了青楼，花魁下了轿子就告诉了朱重自己一直藏在心里的秘密：她一直努力把自己赚的钱存起来，等找到真心爱她一辈子的情郎就从青楼赎身出去。从那天以后，朱重和花魁就快乐地在一起生活了。

　　可想而知，城里所有的绅士们听到小小的卖油郎现在独占了花魁都惊得目瞪口呆。不过呢，"人不可貌相"的说法是千真万确的。实际上，朱重本来也是来自开封府的一户好人家。女真族灭了北宋以后，朱重的家庭也被毁了，十三岁的朱重就过继给了没有子女的油店朱老板。大家得知朱重真正的身份以前，都觉得他配不上花魁，现在谁都说他们两个人真是门当户对。

The Chinese Proverb

人	不	可	貌	相,
rén	bù	kě	mào	xiàng
person	not	can	appearance	to appraise, to judge

海	水	不	可	斗	量
hǎi	shuǐ	bù	kě	dǒu	liáng
ocean	water	not	can	dipper	to measure

Literal meaning: People cannot be judged by their appearance, just as the water in the ocean cannot be measured with a dipper.

Connotations: 1) The background and ability of a person cannot be assessed from his appearance. 2) The true qualities of people lie in the unseen. A person's overt attributes such as rank, social status and level of education do not necessarily reveal his or her true character.

The original source: This proverb is so popular that it has appeared in numerous literary works. The source of our story is: "The Oil Peddler Solely Possesses Huakui," in the collection *Stories to Awaken the World*, by Feng Menglong (1574–1646) of the Ming dynasty. 明•冯梦龙 (1574–1646)《醒世恒言•卖油郎独占花魁》

Vocabulary

1.	貌相	màoxiàng	to judge by appearance
2.	斗量	dǒuliáng	to measure in terms of **dǒu** (a unit of measure equivalent to 10 liters)
3.	尊崇	zūnchóng	to hold in high esteem, to revere
4.	名妓	míngjì	courtesan
5.	古典	gǔdiǎn	classical
6.	熏陶	xūntáo	to be cultivated through long assimilation
7.	高雅	gāoyǎ	elegant, classy
8.	伴侣	bànlǚ	companion, escort
9.	京城	jīngchéng	walled capital city in imperial times
10.	府	fǔ	seat of government (suffixed to names of capital cities)

11.	出色	chūsè	outstanding
12.	优雅	yōuyǎ	elegant
13.	才女	cáinǚ	talented lady
14.	擅长	shàncháng	to be skilled in
15.	女红刺绣	nǚhóng cìxiù	needlework and embroidery
16.	吟诗作赋	yínshī zuòfù	to recite and compose poetry
17.	琴棋书画	qín qí shū huà	*qín* (a string instrument), chess, calligraphy, painting
18.	宠爱	chǒng'ài	to be doted upon
19.	独生女	dúshēng nǚ	single-child daughter
20.	女真族	Nǚzhēn zú	Jurchen tribe
21.	攻打	gōngdǎ	to attack
22.	毁	huǐ	to destroy
23.	政权	zhèngquán	regime, political power
24.	搬迁	bānqiān	to relocate
25.	百姓	bǎixìng	ordinary citizens
26.	逃往	táowǎng	to flee to
27.	逃难	táonàn	to flee disaster, to become refugees
28.	混乱	hùnluàn	chaos
29.	走散	zǒusàn	to wander off
30.	烟花巷	yānhuā xiàng	red-light district
31.	青楼	qīnglóu	courtesan's quarters, a brothel
32.	红	hóng	popular, hot
33.	鸨娘	bǎoniáng	procuress, madam (of a brothel)
34.	费用	fèiyòng	fee
35.	白银	báiyín	silver
36.	慕名	mùmíng	to admire someone/something due to its reputation
37.	排起…长龙	páiqǐ...chánglóng	to form a long queue
38.	嫖客	piáokè	client of a courtesan/prostitute
39.	有钱有势	yǒuqián yǒushì	to have money and power

40. 穷小子	qióng xiǎozi	poor chap
41. 并非	bìngfēi	by no means not (double negative)
42. 动···念头	dòng...niàntóu	to have the fancy of...
43. 卖油郎	mài yóu láng	a man who sells cooking oil
44. 美貌	měimào	beautiful looks
45. 倾倒	qīngdǎo	to be bowled over
46. 度过	dùguò	to pass (a time period)
47. 甘心	gānxīn	to be content
48. 加倍	jiābèi	to redouble (one's effort)
49. 干活儿	gànhuór	to work (colloquial)
50. 铜板	tóngbǎn	coins
51. 攒够	zǎn'gòu	to save up enough
52. 怯生生地	qièshēngshēngde	timidly
53. 银铺	yínpù	silver shop
54. 兑换	duìhuàn	to exchange (money)
55. 伙计	huǒji	shop clerk
56. 执着	zhízhuó	tenacity, perseverance
57. 感动	gǎndòng	to be moved
58. 再三推托	zàisān tuītuō	to put off repeatedly
59. 打扮	dǎbàn	to dress up
60. 体面	tǐmiàn	dignified
61. 绅士	shēnshì	gentleman
62. 配得上	pèideshàng	to be worthy of ...
63. 接待	jiēdài	to receive (a guest or client)
64. 常客	chángkè	frequent or usual customer
65. 期待	qīdài	to anticipate
66. 喝醉	hēzuì	to be drunk
67. 本性	běnxìng	inherent quality, natural instinct
68. 善良	shànliáng	good and kind
69. 烂泥	lànní	mud, slush

70.	扶	**fú**	to support (with the hand)
71.	盖···被子	**gài...bèizi**	to cover with a quilt
72.	服侍	**fúshi**	to wait upon, to attend to (someone)
73.	告别	**gàobié**	to bid goodbye
74.	补觉	**bǔjiào**	to make up for lost sleep
75.	凌乱	**língluàn**	disheveled
76.	哭泣	**kūqì**	to weep, to sob
77.	定睛一看	**dìng jīng yí kàn**	to fix one's eyes on ...
78.	惊呆	**jīngdāi**	to be startled
79.	拒绝	**jùjué**	to reject
80.	非礼	**fēilǐ**	rudeness
81.	冒犯	**màofàn**	to offend
82.	甩	**shuǎi**	to toss
83.	轿夫	**jiàofū**	sedan chair carrier
84.	护送	**hùsòng**	to escort
85.	藏	**cáng**	to hide
86.	秘密	**mìmì**	secret
87.	存	**cún**	to store up
88.	情郎	**qíngláng**	lover (man)
89.	赎身	**shúshēn**	to redeem oneself, to buy back one's freedom
90.	独占	**dúzhàn**	to have sole possession of ...
91.	目瞪口呆	**mùdèng kǒudāi**	to be dumbstruck
92.	千真万确	**qiānzhēn wànquè**	to be absolutely true and accurate
93.	灭	**miè**	to destroy
94.	过继	**guòjì**	to be adopted as a son into another family
95.	身份	**shēnfen**	status
96.	门当户对	**méndāng hùduì**	well-matched in social and economic status

Laszlo the Janitor

In the early 1980s when I was a professor at a small college and a single mother with two school-age children, I enjoyed working late in my office, because that was the one time of the day when my world was quiet and I could think without interruption. On most days, by the time I left my office, the only other person in the building was a janitor named Laszlo, and the two of us developed a special rapport. We didn't speak much because Laszlo's English was quite limited. Laszlo didn't resemble an ordinary janitor; his attire and demeanor were a bit too formal and he enjoyed his work a bit too much. And most curiously, he would always have a faint smile on his face as though he had some amusing thought in his head as he swept the floor with a melodic rhythm. Then one day another man replaced Laszlo as janitor, and I started missing him. I then found out that he had joined a renowned orchestra as a cello player! As it turned out, he had come to the U.S. with his wife when she got a job teaching piano at my college. Both of them had been with Czechoslovakia's National Symphony Orchestra! When I discovered Laszlo's background, I felt so honored and privileged to have known this accomplished yet humble man.

Since then, I've often had similar encounters with recent immigrants. The most recent one was an Uber driver who had been a physician in Cuba. He and his wife sacrificed their careers and status in Cuba in order to give their daughters a chance for a better future. I've always known not to judge people by their looks, but now I also know that the backgrounds of immigrants cannot be presumed from their status in their adopted country.

新移民给我的启示

八十年代初，我在一所学院当教授，也是带着两个孩子的单亲母亲。我喜欢在办公室里工作到傍晚，因为每天只有那个时候，我的世界才安静下来，我也才能一个人静静地思考。通常，等我离开办公室的时候，大楼里剩下的另一个人就是清洁工拉斯洛了。时间长了，我们两人之间建立了一种默契。我们很少交谈，因为拉斯洛的英文水平很有限。拉斯洛不像普通的清洁工，因为他的衣服和动作总有一点太正式，工作也有点太积极了。最奇特的一点是他脸上总是带着淡淡的微笑，好像他的脑子里想着一些有趣的事，而且在扫地的时候，他的动作总带着一种节奏。有一天，大楼里换了一个清洁工，我开始想念起拉斯洛来了。不久，我就听说拉斯洛其实是一位大提琴高手，最近加入了一个有名的交响乐团！原来，拉斯洛的妻子受聘于我校，担任钢琴教师，而拉斯洛就跟着妻子到美国来了。他们夫妻二人原先都是捷克国家交响乐团的团员！知道了拉斯洛的背景以后，我觉得认识一位这么有成就又这么谦逊的人实在很荣幸。

从那以后，我经常碰到类似拉斯洛一样的新移民。最近的一次是一位优步司机，他来美国以前在古巴是一位医生。他和妻子牺牲了自己的事业与地位，为的是给女儿们创造一个更好的未来。一直以来，我都知道人不可貌相，现在我也知道不能从新移民在美国社会里的地位来断定他们之前的背景。

Vocabulary

97.	启示	**qǐshì**	revelation, inspiration
98.	单亲	**dānqīn**	single parent
99.	傍晚	**bàngwǎn**	nightfall
100.	思考	**sīkǎo**	to think deeply
101.	剩下	**shèngxià**	to remain
102.	清洁工	**qīngjiégōng**	janitor
103.	默契	**mòqì**	tacit understanding, unspoken rapport
104.	有限	**yǒuxiàn**	limited
105.	正式	**zhèngshì**	formal, official
106.	积极	**jījí**	enthusiastic, positive
107.	淡淡的	**dàndànde**	faint
108.	扫地	**sǎodì**	to sweep the floor
109.	节奏	**jiézòu**	rhythm
110.	大提琴	**dàtíqín**	cello
111.	高手	**gāoshǒu**	master (of something)
112.	交响乐团	**jiāoxiǎng yuètuán**	symphony orchestra
113.	受聘于	**shòupìnyú**	to be employed by
114.	担任	**dānrèn**	to serve as
115.	捷克	**Jiékè**	Czechoslovakia
116.	背景	**bèijǐng**	background
117.	成就	**chéngjiù**	accomplishments
118.	谦逊	**qiānxùn**	modest
119.	荣幸	**róngxìng**	honored and fortunate
120.	类似	**lèisì**	similar to
121.	移民	**yímín**	immigrant
122.	优步	**Yōubù**	Uber
123.	古巴	**Gǔbā**	Cuba
124.	牺牲	**xīshēng**	to sacrifice
125.	创造	**chuàngzào**	to create
126.	断定	**duàndìng**	to conclude, to determine

Discussion questions (discuss in English or Chinese):

1. The concept expressed by the Chinese proverb in this chapter is certainly not unique to Chinese culture. Can you think of aphorisms or stories in other cultures that express the same idea?

2. Do you consider yourself a good judge of human character? Can you think of cases where your judgments were either spot on or dead wrong?

3. Applying to any key job these days requires a dossier and personal interview. While a face-to-face meeting with a candidate can be very informative, an employer must not gauge a person by his looks. What else can an employer do to make sure that he has not missed any skeletons in the closet?

Uprooting Sprouts to Help Them Grow

Over two thousand years ago in the State of Song, there was a farmer who worried about his crops not growing fast enough. When the seeds that he planted first sprouted, he was delighted and he went to the field every day to inspect the sprouts to see how much they had grown. But each day he was disappointed that the sprouts hadn't grown much taller. On the fifth day he began pacing back and forth on the edge of his field, scratching his head and thinking to himself, "I've got to think of a way to help them grow!" The next day he finally had an idea. He ran into the field and one by one gave each sprout a little upward tug. It took him from sunrise until sunset to finish this task and he was thoroughly exhausted by it. When he got home he excitedly told his family, "I really wore myself out today, but the effort was well worth it, because I helped each sprout grow quite a lot." His son was alarmed when he heard this, so he rushed out to the field to take a look. Sure enough, all the sprouts had gone limp.

The proverb "pulling up sprouts to help them grow" has come to describe someone who cannot wait for something to develop at its natural pace so he ratchets up the pace through artificial means, with dire consequences. The moral behind this proverb couldn't be more obvious. And yet how many people who are overly impatient and overzealous—such as all those "tiger mothers" in China—ever realize their own folly?

Another question to ask is why the author of this story—the great humanist philosopher Mencius—would write such a humorous parable? Actually, he wanted to use this simple fable to make a point to the feudal rulers of the time and to illustrate for them a deeper concept. Mencius believed that mankind is innately good, and he likened this goodness to water which naturally flows downward. But water can be diverted or even forced to remain on the mountaintop. Likewise, the goodness in human nature can also be disrupted or lost, with the result that we become dominated by negative traits such as resentment, jealousy and deceitfulness. So the caveat to the "innate goodness" of mankind is that it is only

拔苗助长

两千多年前，宋国有个农夫为了自己种的禾苗长得不够快而发愁。刚开始看到种子发芽的时候，农夫很高兴，于是每天到田间去查看禾苗是不是又长高了。一天天过去了，看到禾苗没长高多少，他很失望。到了第五天，他实在忍不住了，就在田边走来走去，抓耳挠腮又自言自语地说："我一定得想个办法来帮它们长快一点！"有一天，他终于想出了一个主意。农夫很快地跑到田里，把禾苗一棵一棵地往上拔了一点。他从早到晚干了一整天，累得筋疲力尽才收工。回到家里，他兴奋地告诉家人："今天真把我累坏了，但是太值了，因为我帮每一棵禾苗都长高了一点。"农夫的儿子听了大吃一惊，就立刻跑到田间去查看一下。果然，所有的禾苗都枯萎了。

　　"拔苗助长"这个成语用来形容一个人没有耐心等待他人或事物顺其自然地发展，便采取人工的办法来加快其成长，结果反而把事情搞糟了。这个成语背后的道理再明显不过了，然而，中国有多少热切盼望孩子早日成才的"虎妈"会意识到自己的作法是错误的呢？

　　从另一个角度来看，伟大的哲学家孟子为什么要写这么一个幽默的寓言故事呢？实际上，孟子希望通过这个简单的故事来告诉当时各诸侯国的统治者一个比较深刻的道理。孟子相信人性本善，并将人性本善比喻为流往低处的水。不过，流动的水也可以改变方向，甚至可以被截留在山顶上。由此类推，人性的善良也有可能受到干扰或者丢失，其结果就是人往往会表现出怨恨、嫉妒以及欺诈这样的负面特征。因此，人性本善只是一种天生的潜力，需要培育才能

a potential that requires nurturing to be fully realized. If it is not nurtured, it will not come to fruition, just like sprouts that are not watered and weeded. However, if the nurturing is too forceful, it will not be in accordance with the natural flow of human nature and therefore will backfire. Nurturing innate goodness means consistently practicing small acts of kindness, so that it becomes second nature. "Helping" that innate goodness to develop is very different; it means being forcefully and intentionally virtuous, as though one has some ulterior motive. It also means being zealous about one's righteousness, which creates resentment in others and bitterness in oneself.

Mencius lived in the era of "a hundred flowers bloom; a hundred schools of thought contend"—when widely different philosophies competed for believers. Given that this era was also fraught with warfare and chaos, Mencius' idealistic views about human nature naturally drew many skeptics. Today, his ideals still have many believers as well as detractors, but the proverb derived from his parable has remained popular in Chinese culture.

生成。没有精心培育，人性本善的特征就不能开花结果，就像不给禾苗浇水锄草的话，它就不能茁壮成长一样。然而，后天的"培育"过分用力的话，也会与人内在的自然生长不协调，产生事与愿违的后果。培育人"内在的善"意味着持续不断地累积小善，使其自然而然地成为第二天性。但如果以"拔苗助长"的方式来培育内在的善，那就会变成一种强制性或刻意的品德高尚，就好像这个人的行为是受外部因素的影响，而不是发自内心的自然流露。这种培育方法还会使一个人过度自诩为正人君子，让别人反感，也造成自己内心苦涩。

孟子生活在"百花齐放，百家争鸣"的时代。当时，不同流派的哲学思想相互竞争来吸引信徒。此外，在那个充满战乱的时代背景下，自然会有许多人质疑孟子关于人性本善的理想主义观点。今天，孟子的思想仍然有很多人赞同，也有不少人质疑，不过出自孟子寓言故事的"拔苗助长"已经成为了中国文化中最常用的成语之一了。

The Chinese Proverb

拔	苗	助	长
bá	**miáo**	**zhù**	**zhǎng**
to pull	sprouts	to help	to grow

Literal meaning: Pulling up sprouts to help them grow.

Connotation: This is a metaphor for someone who is overly anxious to see someone or something develop, and who shortcuts the normal process with extreme measures, to destructive effect.

The original source: "Gongsun Chou, Part I," a chapter in the *Book of Mencius*. Mencius lived 372–289 BCE. The book bearing his name was most likely assembled by his disciples ca. 300 BCE. 《孟子•公孙丑上》（约公元前300年由孟子弟子们编辑）。孟子在世于公元前372 – 289年。

Vocabulary

1.	农夫	**nóngfū**	farmer
2.	禾苗	**hémiáo**	grain seedling
3.	发愁	**fāchóu**	worried, anxious
4.	种子	**zhǒngzi**	seeds
5.	发芽	**fāyá**	to sprout
6.	田间	**tiánjiān**	in the fields
7.	失望	**shīwàng**	disappointed
8.	忍不住	**rěnbuzhù**	cannot bear it (anymore)
9.	抓耳挠腮	**zhuāěr náosāi**	lit. "to pull the ear and scratch the cheek"
10.	自言自语	**zìyán zìyǔ**	talking to oneself
11.	筋疲力尽	**jīnpílìjìn**	utterly exhausted
12.	收工	**shōugōng**	to quit work
13.	兴奋	**xīngfèn**	excited
14.	值	**zhí**	worthwhile
15.	大吃一惊	**dàchī yìjīng**	greatly shocked

16. 枯萎	kūwěi	withered
17. 形容	xíngróng	to describe
18. 耐心	nàixīn	patience
19. 等待	děngdài	to wait
20. 他人	tārén	other people
21. 顺其自然	shùn qí zìrán	to let nature take its course
22. 采取	cǎiqǔ	to adopt (a method)
23. 人工	réngōng	artificial
24. 反而	fǎn'ér	on the contrary
25. 再…不过了	zài...búguòle	cannot be more ...
26. 明显	míngxiǎn	obvious
27. 热切	rèqiè	fervent, earnest
28. 盼望	pànwàng	to hope, to long for
29. 成才	chéngcái	to become accomplished
30. 错误	cuòwù	mistake
31. 角度	jiǎodù	angle, perspective
32. 哲学家	zhéxuéjiā	philosopher
33. 幽默	yōumò	humorous
34. 寓言	yùyán	parable
35. 诸侯国	zhūhóuguó	feudal state
36. 统治者	tǒngzhìzhě	ruler
37. 人性本善	rénxìng běn shàn	humans are good by nature
38. 比喻	bǐyù	analogy, metaphor
39. 截留	jiéliú	to block and retain, to hold up
40. 由此类推	yóu cǐ lèituī	along the same line of reasoning
41. 善良	shànliáng	good and kind; goodness
42. 干扰	gānrǎo	to disturb; disturbance
43. 丢失	diūshī	to be lost
44. 怨恨	yuànhèn	resentment, hatred
45. 嫉妒	jìdù	envy, jealousy
46. 欺诈	qīzhà	to deceive; deceitfulness

47. 负面	fùmiàn	negative
48. 特征	tèzhēng	characteristic
49. 天生	tiānshēng	inborn, innate
50. 潜力	qiánlì	potential
51. 培育	péiyù	to cultivate, to nurture
52. 精心	jīngxīn	painstakingly
53. 开花结果	kāihuā jiéguǒ	to blossom and bear fruit
54. 浇水锄草	jiāoshuǐ chúcǎo	to water (the plants) and hoe weeds
55. 茁壮	zhuózhuàng	sturdy
56. 内在	nèizài	internal
57. 协调	xiétiáo	in harmony, in accord
58. 事与愿违	shì yǔ yuàn wéi	things go contrary to one's wishes
59. 意味着	yìwèizhe	to imply, to mean
60. 累积	lěijī	to accumulate
61. 自然而然	zìrán érrán	naturally; in due course
62. 第二天性	dì'èr tiānxìng	second nature
63. 强制性	qiángzhìxìng	mandatory, by force
64. 刻意	kèyì	intentionally

....

The Proverb in Modern Usage

Cultivating Musical Talent

I don't think of myself as a tiger mom, but I must admit I have made the mistake of "helping a sprout grow by pulling on it." The small academic community in which I raised my two children offered many opportunities to nurture their academic and extracurricular interests. So when my son started banging on the piano at age three, I took that as a sign that he was ready for piano lessons. I found a wonderful teacher who specialized in the Suzuki method, which is based on the premise that learning a musical instrument is akin to acquiring one's mother tongue, and is there-

65. 品德高尚	pǐndé gāoshàng	lofty character, righteousness
66. 行为	xíngwéi	behavior
67. 因素	yīnsù	factor
68. 发自内心	fāzì nèixīn	to emanate from the heart
69. 流露	liúlù	to reveal
70. 自诩	zìxǔ	to brag
71. 正人君子	zhèngrén jūnzǐ	man of honor
72. 反感	fǎn'gǎn	antipathy
73. 苦涩	kǔsè	bitter
74. 百花齐放，百家争鸣	bǎihuā qífàng, bǎijiā zhēngmíng	a hundred flowers bloom; a hundred schools of thought contend
75. 流派	liúpài	school (of thought), sect
76. 信徒	xìntú	believers, adherents
77. 充满	chōngmǎn	to be filled with
78. 战乱	zhànluàn	war and chaos
79. 背景	bèijǐng	background
80. 质疑	zhìyí	to call in question, to challenge
81. 赞同	zàntóng	to agree with, to endorse

:::

成语今用实例

培养孩子的音乐天赋

我不认为自己是个虎妈，不过也得承认曾经犯过"拔苗助长"的错误。我是在一个学术氛围浓厚的小社区里把两个孩子养育成人的，而那样的地方有很多的机会培养孩子们的兴趣爱好。在儿子满了三岁，开始乒乒乓乓地敲打钢琴的时候，我就以为儿子可以开始学钢琴了。我给他找了一位铃木教学法专家。所谓"铃木教学法"就是主张学习乐器跟自然

fore especially well-suited for young children. This method requires not only loving encouragement at home, but also the total involvement of at least one parent, including attending lessons with the teacher, serving as a home tutor on a daily basis, etc. Since this was a huge investment of my own time, I have wondered if I fell into one-sided wishful thinking.

My son made good progress and so did I! But when it came time for the mandatory group recital, my son—an introvert since early childhood—resisted. Performing well and being applauded did not bring the additional incentive that his teacher and I expected. From then on, the periodic group recitals became a regular ordeal. According to the Suzuki curriculum, when a child reaches the first milestone by completing the first book in the Suzuki series, the occasion is celebrated with a solo recital. But to my son, this solo performance became the straw that broke the camel's back. My son put on an impressive performance and did his teacher proud. But after returning home, he announced that he was quitting piano because he never wanted to be on stage again! Like the farmer who had pulled up his sprouts, I was stunned, but there was nothing I could do at that point.

A couple of years later, one day out of the blue, my son announced that he was taking up the classical guitar with a teacher that he had found for himself. It would not be by the Suzuki method and there would be no recitals. I was ecstatic that my wilted musical sprout had come back to life!

语言习得一样，因而特别适合幼小的儿童。这种教学法要求父母给孩子提供一个充满关爱和鼓励的学习环境，而且父母当中至少有一人得全身心投入，包括跟孩子一起上课，并每天担任孩子练琴的家庭教师。由于时间成本上的巨大投入，我一直以来都在怀疑那个时候我对培养儿子弹钢琴是不是过分地一厢情愿。儿子弹琴进步很快，我也一样！到了例行的小组演奏会时，从小就很内向的儿子开始抗拒了。精彩的演奏和观众的掌声并没有给他带来钢琴老师和我都期待的动力。从此，每一次的小组演奏会都成为了折磨。按照铃木教学法的教程，孩子学完系列教材第一册的时候，就到达了第一阶段的里程碑，因而要举办一场独奏音乐会来庆祝一下。但是对我儿子来说这场庆祝演奏会却成为了"压垮骆驼的最后一根稻草"。儿子的表演很精彩，也让他的老师感到很骄傲。然而，我们一回到家，儿子就宣布不再弹钢琴了，因为他再也不想上台表演了！当时我就像那位拔苗助长的农夫一样，目瞪口呆，什么法子也想不出来了。又过了几年，儿子有一天突然宣布他要开始学习弹奏古典吉他了。他给自己找了一位老师，不采用铃木教学法，也没有演奏会。我顿时欣喜若狂，原来我以为已经枯萎的那棵音乐禾苗又复活了！

Vocabulary

82.	培养	**péiyǎng**	to cultivate
83.	天赋	**tiānfù**	talent, genius
84.	承认	**chéngrèn**	to admit, to confess
85.	犯…错误	**fàn...cuòwù**	to make the mistake of ...
86.	学术	**xuéshù**	academic
87.	氛围	**fēnwéi**	ambience, atmosphere
88.	浓厚	**nónghòu**	dense, thick
89.	社区	**shèqū**	community
90.	养育	**yǎngyù**	to cultivate, to develop
91.	乒乒乓乓	**pīngpīngpāngpāng**	the sound of banging
92.	敲打	**qiāodǎ**	to beat, to tap
93.	铃木教学法	**Língmù jiàoxuéfǎ**	Suzuki teaching method
94.	专家	**zhuānjiā**	expert
95.	所谓	**suǒwèi**	so-called
96.	主张	**zhǔzhāng**	to advocate
97.	乐器	**yuèqì**	musical instrument
98.	习得	**xídé**	to learn, to acquire a skill through practice
99.	幼小	**yòuxiǎo**	young (children)
100.	充满	**chōngmǎn**	to be filled with
101.	鼓励	**gǔlì**	to encourage
102.	全身心	**quán shēnxīn**	total body and mind
103.	投入	**tóurù**	to invest in, to devote to
104.	担任	**dānrèn**	to serve in the role of ...
105.	成本	**chéngběn**	cost; amount of effort, time, or capital invested
106.	怀疑	**huáiyí**	to suspect
107.	一厢情愿	**yìxiāng qíngyuàn**	one-sided wishful thinking
108.	例行	**lìxíng**	routine, regular procedure
109.	演奏会	**yǎnzòuhuì**	musical performance, recital
110.	内向	**nèixiàng**	introverted
111.	抗拒	**kàngjù**	to resist

112.	精彩	**jīngcǎi**	splendid
113.	掌声	**zhǎngshēng**	the sound of clapping, applause
114.	期待	**qīdài**	to anticipate, to look forward to
115.	动力	**dònglì**	incentive, motivation
116.	折磨	**zhémó**	torment, ordeal
117.	按照	**ànzhào**	according to ...
118.	教程	**jiàochéng**	course of study
119.	系列	**xìliè**	series
120.	里程碑	**lǐchéng bēi**	milestone
121.	独奏	**dúzòu**	solo performance (music)
122.	庆祝	**qìngzhù**	to celebrate
123.	压垮骆驼的 最后一根稻草	**yākuǎ luòtuode** **zuìhòu yìgēn dàocǎo**	literal translation of "the straw that broke the camel's back"
124.	骄傲	**jiāo'ào**	proud
125.	宣布	**xuānbù**	to announce
126.	目瞪口呆	**mùdèng kǒudāi**	stupefied, stunned
127.	弹奏	**tánzòu**	to play (a string instrument)
128.	古典吉他	**gǔdiǎn jítā**	classical guitar
129.	采用	**cǎiyòng**	to select for use, to adopt
130.	顿时	**dùnshí**	immediately, at once
131.	欣喜若狂	**xīnxǐ ruòkuáng**	to be wild with joy, ecstatic
132.	复活	**fùhuó**	to return to life, to be revived

Discussion questions (discuss in English or Chinese):

1. Can you think of a real-life example where the proverb "uprooting sprouts to help them grow" can be applied?

2. If you are a parent, how would you draw the line between encouraging your child to meet his potential and pulling the sprout up to help it grow? If you had to err on one side or the other, which side would you choose?

3. If you believe in Mencius' idea that mankind is innately good, how would you cultivate that innate goodness so that it is not lost or warped?

Keep the Mountain Green
So You'll Have Firewood to Burn

Once upon a time, there was a man who made a living chopping wood from two hillsides that he owned and selling the firewood to folks in the village. His wife died when his two sons were still small, so the boys had to become self-sufficient from a young age. The older boy was named Qingshan ("Green Mountain") and the younger one was called Hongshan ("Red Mountain"). When the boys reached their teens, they also learned to chop wood. The old man worked very hard all his life, right up to the time when he sensed that he may not have much longer to live. At that point, he bequeathed the eastern hillside to Qingshan and the western one to Hongshan. Even though the two boys had always been very close, the old man had the wisdom to divide their inheritance evenly in advance. Within just a few months the old man passed away, fully at peace, knowing that his sons would have a secure future.

The forest on the western hillside was quite dense and the trees cut down from it made excellent firewood. Hongshan had learned to work hard from his father. Every day from morning till night, he chopped wood and sold it in the village. Soon he became quite prosperous. But the trees in the forest were becoming depleted fast. Within five years or so, they were almost all gone, so Hongshan began planting corn on his hillside. All was well until mid-summer, when a horrendous storm hit the area and washed away all the corn stalks before the corn was ready to harvest. He was devastated, so he went to ask his older brother on the east side for help.

The forest on the eastern hillside was originally a bit sparse, but Qingshan laid out a good plan to make the best of its resources. First, he thinned out the trees that would never produce useful timber and sold them as firewood. Then he replaced them with new tree saplings. Next, he plowed the area at the foot of the hill and planted crops there. He also began to raise a few cows and sheep. Life was tough in those first few years, as he barely had enough income to get by. But when the horrendous storm hit, there was hardly any damage to his crops, since they were

留得青山在，
不怕没柴烧

很久以前，一个老人有两座山，生活就靠砍树卖柴给乡亲们来维持。他的妻子在两个儿子还很小的时候就去世了，因此两个小孩从小就得学会自立。大的男孩叫青山，小的叫红山。孩子长成少年以后，也学会了砍树。老人一辈子起早贪黑地劳动，直到有一天他意识到自己活不了太久了。于是他把东边那座山给了青山，西边那座山给了红山。尽管兄弟两人关系很好，老人还是很明智地在生前将遗产平均分配给了两个儿子。老人知道儿子们的将来有了保障，没过几个月就平静地去世了。

西边那座山的森林相当茂密，砍下来的树都是上好的柴。红山像父亲一样辛勤劳动，每天早出晚归，砍树卖柴给乡亲们。不久，他的日子渐渐富裕起来。然而，山上的树也日渐稀疏了。大约五年的时间里，所有的树都被砍光了，红山就在山坡上种起了玉米。一切看起来都还不错。没想到，在夏季的一天，一场大暴雨把丰收在望的玉米全毁了。走投无路的红山只好到东山去投奔哥哥。

东边那座山上的森林原本比较稀疏，不过青山因地制宜，做了周全的规划。首先，他砍掉了一些不能成材的树木，晒成干柴卖掉了。接着他又种了新的树苗。其次，他在山脚开垦耕地，种上了庄稼，还养起了牛羊。头几年，青山的日子过得紧巴巴的。不过，那场大暴雨来临的时候，青山的庄稼几乎没受到什么影响，因为山上的植被起到了很好的保护

protected by the forest above. After the storm passed, Qingshan's fields were lush and green, and a rainbow arched over the forest.

When Hongshan arrived at Qingshan's place, he was astonished at what he saw, so he asked his brother how it had become so lush. Qingshan put his hand on his brother's shoulder and replied affectionately and earnestly, "When you take from the mountain without cultivating it, sooner or later it will be all used up. You have to first cultivate the mountain, and then take from it without depleting it. Only then will the mountain remain forever green."

作用。暴雨过后，庄稼地里郁郁葱葱，一道彩虹出现在森林上空。

　　红山到了青山家，看到眼前的景象顿时惊呆了。他问哥哥这一切是如何做到的。青山搂着弟弟的肩膀，深情而殷切地说：“要是你只从山上索取而不加以耕作，迟早会把山吃空的。你得先耕作，再收获，千万不能把原本的资源耗尽了，这样青山才可以常绿。”

When the villagers found out what had happened to the two brothers' hillsides after the storm, they all exclaimed, "As long as Qingshan is here, we will not have to worry about running out of firewood!"* These words have become a proverb promoting preservation of environmental resources, and the proverb is still sometimes used in that sense today.

Soon after this proverb was created, it also began to be used metaphorically to mean "as long as some life remains, there's hope for a comeback." Later on, this secondary meaning became more widely used, as can be seen in another popular story from the seventeenth century. In this story, a wealthy merchant with extraordinary ambitions named Guo Qilang "purchased" a government post. However, before he arrived at the new post, his hometown was devastated by a rebellion, in which his family's mansion and business were plundered. Everyone in his family except his elderly mother had vanished. Then, in a boat with his mother in tow, on his way to take up the post, they were caught in a devastating storm, from which they narrowly escaped with nothing but their lives. The only thing Guo Qilang could say to comfort his mother was this: "As long as the green mountain is still here, we will not have to worry about running out of firewood. I still have my official position. As long as I can arrive at my post, everything will be fine." What Qilang meant was that his mother should take comfort from the fact that he was still alive, and that he would surely make a comeback. Sadly, the multiple traumas were too much for the old lady and she died soon after. Failing to find his letter of appointment, which was lost in the storm, Qilang soon discovered that all doors were closed to him, and he had to earn a livelihood by becoming a lowly boatman.

---

* Qingshan is a double entendre here. It refers to both the brother Qingshan as well as the forested hillside.

当乡亲们看到暴雨后兄弟俩的山头截然不同的景象时，都感叹道："留得青山在*，不怕没柴烧！"后来，这句话变成了一个谚语，用在促进自然资源保护的语境下，直到今天也还是如此。

然而，这个谚语出现后不久，很快就衍生出了"只要保住性命，就可以东山再起"的寓意。后来，这个新的寓意比谚语的本意使用得更普遍，这从十七世纪广为流传的一个故事就看得出来。故事说的是一个富有而雄心勃勃的商人郭七郎，"买得"了一个衙门的官职。不过他还没有到任，老家就发生了叛乱，而家里的豪宅和生意都毁于叛乱中。除了年老的母亲以外，其他家人也都遇难了。郭七郎带着老母亲，搭船前往衙门赴任。不巧，途中遇到了暴风雨。郭七郎和母亲虽然保住了性命，但已身无分文，一无所有了。郭七郎只能安慰母亲说："留得青山在，不怕没柴烧。我还有衙门的官职。只要我到衙门做了官，一切都会好起来的。"七郎的意思是母亲应该因为他还活着而感到宽慰，而他一定会东山再起的。不幸的是，老母亲经不住这接二连三的灾祸，没过多久就去世了。可怜的郭七郎后来发现，因为官职任命书在暴风雨中丢失了，衙门也都对他关上了大门，最后他只好靠撑船来维持生计了。

---

* 这里的"青山"是一个双关语，既是指兄长青山，亦是指森林茂密的青山。

The Chinese Proverb

留得	青	山	在
liúde	qīng	shān	zài
to retain	green	mountain	to exist

不	怕	没	柴	烧
bú	pà	méi	chái	shāo
not	fear	to have no	firewood	to burn

Literal meaning: Keep the mountain green so you will not have to worry about having no firewood to burn.

Connotations:

1. Preserving our natural environment is the best way to ensure that our natural resources will not run out.
2. As long as there is some life left, we can still make a comeback.
3. As long as there are regenerative resources, there's hope for restoration (traditional words of encouragement after a disaster strikes).

The original source: Slapping the Table in Amazement (A Ming Dynasty Story Collection), Chapter 22. Author: Ling Mengchu (1580–1644)
明 • 凌濛初 《初刻拍案惊奇》 卷二十二

Vocabulary

1.	柴	**chái**	firewood
2.	靠…来…	**kào...lái...**	to rely on ... in order to ...
3.	砍	**kǎn**	to chop (wood)
4.	乡亲们	**xiāngqīnmen**	town folks
5.	维持	**wéichí**	to maintain, to sustain
6.	去世	**qùshì**	to pass away
7.	自立	**zìlì**	to stand on one's own feet, to be self-sufficient
8.	少年	**shàonián**	youth, teenager
9.	起早贪黑	**qǐzǎo tānhēi**	to work from dawn to dusk
10.	意识到	**yìshidào**	to become aware of ...
11.	于是	**yúshì**	thereupon, therefore
12.	明智	**míngzhì**	wise

13.	生前	**shēngqián**	while still alive, before death
14.	遗产	**yíchǎn**	inheritance
15.	平均分配	**píngjūn fēnpèi**	to allocate evenly
16.	保障	**bǎozhàng**	guarantee, safeguard
17.	平静	**píngjìng**	peacefully, quietly
18.	森林	**sēnlín**	forest, jungle
19.	茂密	**màomì**	dense, luxuriant
20.	上好	**shànghǎo**	top-grade
21.	辛勤	**xīnqín**	industrious, hardworking
22.	早出晚归	**zǎochū wǎnguī**	lit. "go out early and return late"; to work from morning 'til night
23.	富裕	**fùyù**	prosperous, well-off
24.	日渐	**rìjiàn**	gradually, day-by-day
25.	稀疏	**xīshū**	sparse
26.	山坡	**shānpō**	slope (of a hill)
27.	玉米	**yùmǐ**	corn
28.	暴雨	**bàoyǔ**	torrential rain
29.	丰收在望	**fēngshōu zàiwàng**	a bumper harvest is anticipated
30.	毁	**huǐ**	to destroy
31.	走投无路	**zǒutóu wúlù**	there is no way out; to be at an impasse
32.	投奔	**tóubèn**	to seek refuge
33.	原本	**yuánběn**	originally
34.	因地制宜	**yīn dì zhì yí**	to adopt measures that fit local conditions
35.	周全	**zhōuquán**	thorough, comprehensive
36.	规划	**guīhuà**	plan, program
37.	首先⋯ 其次⋯	**shǒuxiān...qícì...**	first ..., then ...
38.	成材	**chéngcái**	to grow into useful timber
39.	晒	**shài**	to dry under the sun
40.	树苗	**shùmiáo**	tree saplings
41.	山脚	**shānjiǎo**	foot of a hill
42.	开垦耕地	**kāikěn gēngdì**	to open up arable land

43.	庄稼	**zhuāngjia**	crops
44.	紧巴巴	**jǐnbābā**	tight, hard up
45.	来临	**láilín**	(something unfortunate) to descend on
46.	几乎	**jīhū**	almost
47.	植被	**zhíbèi**	vegetation cover
48.	起…作用	**qǐ...zuòyòng**	to have the effect of ...
49.	郁郁葱葱	**yùyù cōngcōng**	green and luxuriant
50.	彩虹	**cǎihóng**	rainbow
51.	上空	**shàngkōng**	the sky above, overhead
52.	景象	**jǐngxiàng**	scene, scenario
53.	顿时	**dùnshí**	at once
54.	惊呆	**jīngdāi**	stupefied, dumbstruck
55.	搂	**lǒu**	to hug, to hold in one's arm(s)
56.	肩膀	**jiānbǎng**	shoulder
57.	深情	**shēnqíng**	with deep feeling
58.	殷切	**yīnqiè**	ardently
59.	索取	**suǒqǔ**	to extract
60.	耕作	**gēngzuò**	to cultivate, to till
61.	迟早	**chízǎo**	sooner or later
62.	吃空	**chīkōng**	"to eat until it's all gone," to totally deplete
63.	收获	**shōuhuò**	to harvest
64.	资源	**zīyuán**	resources
65.	耗尽	**hàojìn**	to use up
66.	截然不同	**jiérán bùtóng**	to be completely different
67.	感叹	**gǎntàn**	to sigh, to exclaim
68.	谚语	**yànyǔ**	proverb, saying
69.	促进	**cùjìn**	to promote, to spur
70.	语境	**yǔjìng**	context
71.	衍生	**yǎnshēng**	to derive, to generate

72.	性命	**xìngmìng**	life
73.	东山再起	**dōngshān zàiqǐ**	to stage a comeback (idiom)
74.	寓意	**yùyì**	metaphorical meaning
75.	本意	**běnyì**	original meaning
76.	广为流传	**guǎngwéi liúchuán**	to be circulated widely
77.	富有	**fùyǒu**	wealthy
78.	雄心勃勃	**xióngxīn bóbó**	very ambitious
79.	衙门	**yámen**	government office (in olden times)
80.	官职	**guānzhí**	official position
81.	到任	**dàorèn**	to arrive at a post/job
82.	叛乱	**pànluàn**	rebellion
83.	豪宅	**háozhái**	luxurious house
84.	毁于	**huǐyú**	to be destroyed by
85.	遇难	**yùnàn**	killed in a disaster or accident
86.	搭船	**dāchuán**	to take a boat
87.	赴任	**fùrèn**	to go to one's post
88.	不巧	**bùqiǎo**	unfortunately
89.	途中	**túzhōng**	en route
90.	身无分文	**shēnwúfēnwén**	penniless, totally broke
91.	一无所有	**yìwúsuǒyǒu**	to have nothing
92.	安慰	**ānwèi**	to console
93.	宽慰	**kuānwèi**	to be comforted
94.	经不住	**jīngbuzhù**	unable to bear
95.	接二连三	**jiēèr liánsān**	one after another, in quick succession
96.	灾祸	**zāihuò**	disasters
97.	任命书	**rènmìngshū**	letter of appointment
98.	撑船	**chēngchuán**	to punt a boat
99.	生计	**shēngjì**	livelihood
100.	双关语	**shuāngguānyǔ**	a word or phrase with double meaning

Rising from the Ashes of War

With a history of well over a century, the Commercial Press is the oldest existing Chinese publishing company. It was founded in 1897 in Shanghai and is still flourishing today. After 1949, separate branches of this publishing house were established in China, Hong Kong, Taiwan, Singapore and Malaysia. In 1993, these independent operations joined forces to establish Commercial Press International Ltd. This publishing company is familiar to all educated Chinese, but very few know that it would not exist today if it had not survived a devastating attack before the outbreak of World War II.

On January 28, 1932, Japan launched an attack in Shanghai that included bombing from the air. The bombing destroyed the headquarters of the Commercial Press along with its vast collection of rare books stored in the attached Eastern Library. At the time, the Japanese commander of this operation said, "If we destroy a block, they will rebuild it in a year, If we destroy the Eastern Library, the root of thousands of years of Chinese culture will be destroyed."*

The leadership and people behind the publishing house survived and they were determined to rise from the ashes. In the spirit of "keeping the mountain green and not fearing that there will be no more firewood," the Commercial Press resumed operations on August 1, 1932, just six months after the devastating destruction. The leaders of the press also took the rejuvenation as an opportunity to usher in reforms that made the press more resilient to future perils.

---

* bbs.tianya.cn/post-worldlook-1891722-1.shtml

劫后余生的商务印书馆

有着一百多年历史的商务印书馆是中国现存最早的出版社。商务印书馆在1897年成立于上海，到今天还充满活力。1949年以后，商务印书馆在中国大陆、香港、台湾、新加坡以及马来西亚分别建立了分馆。1993年，这些独立运作的分馆联合了起来，成立了商务印书馆国际有限公司。在受过教育的中国人当中，商务印书馆可以说众人皆知，然而却很少有人知道这家赫赫有名的出版社在第二次世界大战爆发前夕的一次破坏性袭击中几乎毁于一旦。

　　1932年1月28日，日本对上海发起了攻击，包括从空中轰炸上海。空袭摧毁了商务印书馆总部，以及与之相连的东方图书馆，而当时馆内藏有大量的善本书籍。担任空袭司令的日本军官称："要是我们炸毁一条街，他们一年之内便可以重建；但是，如果我们炸毁了东方图书馆，将彻底摧毁几千年中华文化的根。"

　　商务印书馆的领导层以及在背后支持出版事业的人们得以劫后余生，励志从灾难中再次崛起。本着"留着青山在，不怕没柴烧"的精神，商务印书馆在空袭后仅仅六个月，于1932年8月1日恢复了运营。馆里的领导层也利用这次复兴的机会进行了一系列改革，以使商务印书馆在面对未来可能发生的灾难时更有活力。

Vocabulary

101.	劫后余生	jiéhòu yúshēng	to survive a disaster
102.	现存	xiàncún	extant
103.	出版社	chūbǎnshè	publishing house
104.	充满活力	chōngmǎn huólì	to be full of vitality
105.	分别	fēnbié	separately, respectively
106.	运作	yùnzuò	to operate, to carry out its functions
107.	众人皆知	zhòngrén jiēzhī	everyone knows
108.	赫赫有名	hèhè yǒumíng	renowned, illustrious
109.	爆发	bàofā	to break out
110.	前夕	qiánxī	on the eve of ..., just before ...
111.	破坏性	pòhuàixìng	destructive
112.	袭击	xíjī	to attack by surprise
113.	毁于一旦	huǐyú yídàn	to be destroyed in one day
114.	攻击	gōngjī	to attack
115.	轰炸	hōngzhà	to bomb
116.	空袭	kōngxí	aerial attack
117.	摧毁	cuīhuǐ	to destroy
118.	总部	zǒngbù	headquarters
119.	与之相连	yǔzhī xiānglián	to be connected with it
120.	藏有	cángyǒu	to have in its holdings
121.	善本书籍	shànběn shūjí	rare books
122.	担任	dānrèn	to be in the role of, to serve as
123.	司令	sīlìng	commander
124.	炸毁	zhàhuǐ	to destroy by bombing
125.	彻底	chèdǐ	thoroughgoing, comprehensive, exhaustive
126.	根	gēn	roots
127.	领导层	lǐngdǎocéng	the leadership level
128.	励志	lìzhì	to be determined to ...
129.	灾难	zāinàn	disaster

130.	崛起	**juéqǐ**	to rise up
131.	本着···的精神	**běnzhe...de jīngshén**	(do something) in line with the spirit of ...
132.	恢复	**huīfù**	to recover, to recuperate
133.	运营	**yùnyíng**	to put into operation
134.	复兴	**fùxīng**	to rejuvenate, to revive
135.	一系列	**yí xìliè**	a series of ...

Discussion questions (discuss in English or Chinese):

1. The proverb "keep the mountain green and we will have no fear of not having firewood to burn" is literally about forest protection. The story of Noah's Ark is about preserving the animal kingdom in a massive flood. How would you relate the story of Noah's Ark to the proverb?

2. Nelson Mandela, Nobel laureate and international icon of democracy and social justice, was at one time sentenced to life imprisonment in his home country of South Africa. In the end, he served a total of 27 years in prison. How does the proverb in this chapter apply to his life?

3. Can you think of a scenario or a personal story which can be appropriately summarized by the proverb in this chapter?

Covering One's Ears to Steal a Bell

In the late Spring and Autumn period (ca. 550 BCE), six powerful clans within the feudal state of Jin were struggling for supremacy. When the Zhao clan annihilated the Fan clan, thieves took the opportunity to loot the Fan mansion. One of the thieves was attracted by a large bell hanging in the courtyard.* He could tell that it was extremely valuable because it was made of high-grade bronze. Its shape and surface pattern were exquisite. The thief first tried to carry the bell out in one piece, but it was too heavy and he couldn't budge it an inch. After racking his brains a bit, he thought of a way. He would break it up into pieces and carry the pieces one by one to his house. So he went home to get a sledge hammer. With one swing of the hammer came an ear-splitting clang, which so alarmed the thief that he instinctively wrapped his arms around the bell to silence it. This only made the rumble—which was reverberating throughout the town—run through his whole body. So by reflex, his hands flew to his ears in shock, whereupon the rumble was instantly muffled. This brought the thief a happy thought, "Aha, I can stuff my ears with cotton and go on breaking up the bell!" Clang, clang, clang, the deafening sound reverberated far and wide. In no time, a huge crowd gathered and the brainless thief was arrested.

The reader might wonder how an absurd parable has become a popular proverb in Chinese culture. Well, as with all parables, this one has a deep philosophical message. The story comes from the *Annals of Lü* (ca.

---

* The English word "bell" can refer to something as large as the American Liberty Bell or as small as a bicycle bell. In Chinese, the large bells are called 钟 **zhōng**, and they are struck from the outside; the small bells are called 铃 **líng**, and they are rung from the inside. This story is about stealing a 钟 **zhōng**. The original proverb was 掩耳盗钟 "**yǎn ěr dào zhōng**," but it has morphed to 掩耳盗铃 "**yǎn ěr dào líng**."

掩耳盗铃

春秋末年（约公元前550年），晋国六大家族相互争霸。当赵氏灭掉范氏以后，一群小偷趁机闯进范氏大院盗窃财物。一个小偷看中了挂在院子里的一口大钟[*]。小偷很识货，看出来这口钟是用上等青铜铸成的，形状和钟面又很精美，肯定非常值钱。小偷本来想把整口钟搬回家，可是他用尽力气，钟还是一点儿也挪不动。小偷想来想去，想到了一个办法。他决定把钟敲成碎块，然后一块一块地搬回家，于是小偷就回家去拿了一个大锤子。回到院子里，小偷抡起那个大锤子在大钟上敲了一下，"砰!!!"的一声，大钟发出了震耳欲聋的响声。小偷吓了一跳，本能地张开双臂抱住了大钟，想要摁住响声。没想到震颤的大钟发出的响声回荡在整个镇子里，让小偷觉得心都快被震出来了。惊慌中，他的双手不由自主地捂住了耳朵，而隆隆的钟声立刻听不清了。小偷高兴了起来："太好了，我可以用布块把耳朵塞上，然后再把钟敲碎！"接下来，"砰! 砰! 砰! "的钟声响彻云霄。不一会儿，一群乡亲们就赶到范氏大院里，把这个脑残的小偷抓起来了。

读者可能觉得很奇怪，那么荒诞的一个寓言故事怎么会成为了中国文化中最常用的一个成语呢？其实，跟所有的寓言故事一样，"掩耳盗铃"也包含了深刻的哲学道理。这个故

---

[*] 英文词"bell"可以指如美国自由钟那么大的钟，也可以指像自行车上的铃铛那么小的铃。在中文里，大的称为钟，通常是从外面敲，而小的叫作铃，一般从里面摇。这个成语的原意是"掩耳盗钟，"但后来演变为"掩耳盗铃"了。

239 BCE), a compendium of writings from all fields of scholarship, but primarily history and philosophy. One dominant theme was "how to be a good ruler," the number one concern of scholars at a time rife with strife and chaos.

In its original context, the parable about the brainless thief was preceded by a preamble asserting that the most pernicious failing of contemporary rulers was being ignorant of their own shortcomings. This assertion is substantiated by a long list of concrete examples. In contrast to the rulers of the time, all the wise kings of the Golden Age understood that it is human nature to be blind to one's own faults, all the more so

事出自《吕氏春秋》，一部集合了各家学派、以历史哲学为主的汇编著作。当时（约公元前239年）各个诸侯国之间冲突不断，混乱不堪，文人们最为关切的就是"国君如何成为一位明君"，而这一主题贯穿了整部《吕氏春秋》。

在"掩耳盗铃"的原文中，作者在讲述愚蠢的小偷盗窃大钟的故事之前，首先论述了当代君王最大的失误就是不了解自己的过失。作者一一列举了诸多君王的具体事例来证明自

when one is a lofty ruler. Therefore, they set up mechanisms and advisors to warn them of their errors. Rulers in more recent times not only lacked these safeguards but even deliberately covered their own eyes and ears, leading to disastrous results. The parable ends with the words: "For the thief to avoid having others hear the clang of the bell is understandable, but to avoid hearing it himself is absurd. And yet isn't this exactly how present-day rulers are behaving when they detest hearing about their own faults?"

As the writer was still afraid that his message would fall on deaf ears, he added a recent episode in which a clever advisor manipulated a ruler to convince him to listen to critical advice. In this story, Duke Wen of Wei held a banquet and invited all his officials to voice their opinions of him. Of course, several began by saying how kind, righteous, enlightened, etc., he was. When it came Ren Zuo's turn, he candidly said that the Duke was an unworthy ruler, then proceeded to explain why he thought so. As the Duke's face turned purple with anger, Ren Zuo knew it was time for him to leave.

It was Zhai Huang's turn next and he said, "My lord, you are a wise ruler. I have heard that when a ruler is wise, his advisors will speak candidly. The fact that Ren Zuo has spoken candidly proves that you are wise." This restored the Duke's good humor, so he asked, "Can we get Ren Zuo to come back?" Zhai Huang replied, "Of course! I have heard that a loyal servant will do his utmost to be loyal, even to the point of risking death. Ren Zuo is most likely still right outside the door." Zhai Huang stepped out and sure enough he found Ren Zuo standing there. When Zhai Huang led Ren Zuo back in, the Duke stepped down to receive him, and from that day on treated Ren Zuo like an honored guest. If it were not for Zhai Huang, the Duke would have lost his most loyal servant!

己的观点。相对当时的君王，古代圣明的君王非常了解无视自己的过失是人的本性，何况高高在上的君王。因此，这些明君都采取了某种机制和任用辅弼来提醒自己的过失。近代的君王不但没有建立类似的保险机制，甚至还刻意对自己的过失视而不见，充耳不闻，以至于造成灾难性的后果。作者在寓言故事的结尾写道："小偷不愿意别人听到钟声是可以理解的，但是自己不愿意听到就可笑了。然而，当今的君王不愿意听到自己的过失，不正是跟盗钟的小偷一样吗？"

　　说到这里，作者似乎仍然担心他的观点不会被接受，就接着引用了一个最近的事例，说的是一位聪明的辅弼巧妙地利用了人的本性让君王回心转意，接受了另一位士大夫的批评建议。故事是这样的：魏文侯设宴款待士大夫，并让大家评论自己。于是一些士大夫们都开始赞扬魏文侯，说他如何仁义，正直和英明等等。轮到任座说话的时候，他直率地说魏文侯是一个不肖的君王，并说明了他这个观点的原因。看到魏文侯的脸都气紫了，任座知道他应该退下了。

　　这时候轮到了翟黄，他说："大王，你是一位明君。我听说如果君王圣明，他的大夫们就敢于直言。刚才任座敢于直言正是因为大王很圣明。"魏文侯听到翟黄的话又高兴起来，于是问道："我们还可以让任座回来吗？"翟黄回答说："当然了！我听说忠臣会竭尽全力忠于君王，即使因此会被判死罪也在所不辞。任座很可能还等在外面。"翟黄走出去一看，果然任座还站在那里。翟黄把任座带进宫殿的时候，魏文侯从君王宝座上走下来迎接他，从此待任座如上宾。要不是因为翟黄的一席话，魏文侯可能就失去了一位最忠心的大夫。

The Chinese Proverb

掩	耳	盗	铃
yǎn	ěr	dào	líng
to cover	ears	to steal	a bell

Literal meaning: Covering one's ears to steal a bell.

Connotation: The perpetrator of a misdeed deliberately makes himself oblivious to it. The misdeed is blatant to everyone else but the perpetrator himself.

The original source: *Annals of Lü* (ca. 239 BCE), the chapter "Knowing Oneself" 《吕氏春秋 • 自知》(约公元前239年)

Vocabulary

1.	春秋	**Chūnqiū**	Spring and Autumn (an ancient era in China)
2.	末年	**mònián**	final years (of an era)
3.	家族	**jiāzú**	clan
4.	争霸	**zhēngbà**	to vie for hegemony
5.	氏	**shì**	surname of a clan; "house of ..."
6.	灭掉	**mièdiào**	to annihilate
7.	趁机	**chènjī**	to take advantage of an opportunity
8.	闯进	**chuǎngjìn**	to break into
9.	盗窃	**dàoqiè**	to steal
10.	财物	**cáiwù**	valuable goods
11.	看中	**kànzhòng**	to set one's eye on ...
12.	识货	**shíhuò**	to know a good thing when one sees it
13.	上等	**shàngděng**	first class, top quality
14.	青铜	**qīngtóng**	bronze
15.	铸成	**zhùchéng**	to cast into (re an existing metal object); to be cast from (some material)
16.	形状	**xíngzhuàng**	shape
17.	精美	**jīngměi**	exquisite

18.	挪不动	nuóbudòng	unable to budge
19.	敲成	qiāochéng	to strike/smash into
20.	碎块	suìkuài	fragments
21.	锤子	chuízi	hammer
22.	抡起	lūnqǐ	to begin brandishing
23.	砰	pēng	Bang!
24.	震耳欲聋	zhèn'ěr yùlóng	ear-splitting, deafening
25.	吓了一跳	xiàle yítiào	to be startled, to have a great fright
26.	本能	běnnéng	instinctively
27.	张开双臂	zhāngkāi shuāngbì	to open up both arms
28.	摁住	ènzhù	to press/hold down
29.	震颤	zhènchàn	to tremble
30.	回荡	huídàng	to reverberate, to resound
31.	惊慌	jīnghuāng	alarmed, frightened
32.	不由自主	bùyóu zìzhǔ	involuntarily
33.	捂住	wǔzhù	to cover over, to muffle
34.	隆隆	lónglóng	rumbling sound
35.	响彻云霄	xiǎngchè yúnxiāo	resounding through the skies
36.	乡亲们	xiāngqīnmen	townspeople
37.	脑残	nǎocán	mentally handicapped
38.	荒诞	huāngdàn	absurd
39.	寓言故事	yùyán gùshi	parable (story)
40.	包含	bāohán	to contain
41.	深刻	shēnkè	profound
42.	哲学道理	zhéxué dàolǐ	philosophical principle
43.	以…为主	yǐ...wéizhǔ	to take ... as primary
44.	汇编著作	huìbiān zhùzuò	compiled writings
45.	诸侯国	zhūhóuguó	feudal states
46.	冲突	chōngtū	conflict
47.	混乱不堪	hùnluàn bùkān	to be in utter disorder; chaotic
48.	关切	guānqiè	to be deeply concerned

49.	明君	**míngjūn**	enlightened ruler
50.	贯穿	**guànchuān**	to run through, to permeate
51.	讲述	**jiǎngshù**	to narrate
52.	愚蠢	**yúchǔn**	stupid, foolish
53.	论述	**lùnshù**	to expound
54.	失误	**shīwù**	failing, fault
55.	过失	**guòshī**	mistake
56.	一一列举	**yīyī lièjǔ**	to list one by one
57.	具体	**jùtǐ**	concrete
58.	事例	**shìlì**	instance, example
59.	圣明	**shèngmíng**	wise, sagacious
60.	无视	**wúshì**	to disregard, to be blind to
61.	何况	**hékuàng**	not to mention ..., let alone ...
62.	采取	**cǎiqǔ**	to adopt (a method for doing something)
63.	机制	**jīzhì**	mechanism
64.	任用	**rènyòng**	to appoint
65.	辅弼	**fǔbì**	prime minister, highest assistant to the ruler
66.	类似	**lèisì**	similar
67.	保险机制	**bǎoxiǎn jīzhì**	safeguard, safety mechanism
68.	刻意	**kèyì**	deliberately
69.	视而不见	**shì ér bújiàn**	to turn a blind eye
70.	充耳不闻	**chōngěr bùwén**	to turn a deaf ear
71.	灾难性	**zāinànxìng**	disastrous
72.	后果	**hòuguǒ**	result, outcome
73.	结尾	**jiéwěi**	ending, conclusion
74.	似乎	**sìhū**	seems to

75.	仍然	*réngrán*	still
76.	引用	*yǐnyòng*	to cite
77.	巧妙	*qiǎomiào*	ingenuous
78.	回心转意	*huíxīn zhuǎnyì*	to come around (to correctness)
79.	士大夫	*shìdàfū*	literati, officials (in a ruler's court)
80.	批评建议	*pīpíng jiànyì*	criticisms and suggestions
81.	设宴	*shèyàn*	to put on a banquet
82.	款待	*kuǎndài*	to treat cordially
83.	赞扬	*zànyáng*	to praise
84.	仁义	*rényì*	benevolent
85.	正直	*zhèngzhí*	upright, righteous
86.	英明	*yīngmíng*	sagacious, enlightened
87.	轮到	*lúndào*	to be so-and-so's turn
88.	直率	*zhíshuài*	candid, forthright
89.	不肖	*búxiào*	unworthy
90.	气紫	*qì zǐ*	to turn purple with anger
91.	退下	*tuìxià*	to retreat
92.	敢于直言	*gǎnyú zhíyán*	to dare speak candidly
93.	忠臣	*zhōngchén*	loyal servant (of the ruler)
94.	竭尽全力	*jiéjìn quánlì*	to exert one's utmost effort
95.	判死罪	*pàn sǐzuì*	to be sentenced to death
96.	在所不辞	*zài suǒ bùcí*	will not hesitate to ...
97.	宫殿	*gōngdiàn*	palace
98.	宝座	*bǎozuò*	throne
99.	迎接	*yíngjiē*	to welcome
100.	待…如…	*dài...rú...*	to treat (someone) as ...
101.	上宾	*shàngbīn*	honored guest
102.	一席话	*yìxí huà*	a spiel (formal)

The Massacre at Wounded Knee

The Massacre at Wounded Knee, which occurred in 1890, is an infamous chapter in American history. But it took 100 years for the United States to officially acknowledge its guilt. America's westward expansion in the nineteenth century brought newcomers into direct conflict with the native Sioux Indians. The Sioux were forced to give ground time and time again. The Massacre at Wounded Knee was the final clash between federal troops and the Sioux. In December 1890, the troops rounded up a group of Lakota Indians (one of the three Sioux tribes) on the Lakota Pine Ridge Indian Reservation in South Dakota and proceeded to disarm them. Through a misunderstanding, the disarming was botched and 300 Lakota were massacred, half of them women and children. Twenty-five U.S. Army soldiers also died. In the aftermath, the event was called a "battle" and twenty Medals of Honor—the most prestigious U.S. military award—were awarded to the federal troops. This is a blatant example of "covering one's ears to steal a bell," for any objective observer would have recognized it as a massacre. In 1965, the site was designated a National Historic Landmark. On the centennial of the massacre in 1990, Congress passed a resolution formally expressing "deep regret" for the event. As of 2019, Senator Elizabeth Warren was preparing to introduce a bill to rescind the twenty Medals of Honor awarded at the time.

伤膝溪大屠杀

今天，人们普遍认为1890年发生的伤膝溪大屠杀是美国历史上一起臭名昭著的事件。不过，官方直到惨案发生了100年之后才终于承认了自己的错误。美国从十九世纪开始向西部扩张，使得开拓西部的白人与原住民苏族人之间产生了正面的冲突。苏族人被迫一次又一次从他们的居住地退让出去。伤膝河大屠杀是美国联邦军队与苏族人的最后一次冲突，而这次冲突涉及到的是三支苏族中的拉科塔部落。1890年12月，联邦军队在南达科塔州的拉科塔松岭印第安人保留区包围了一群拉科塔人，并要求他们交出武器。在双方沟通的过程中，因为误会引发了争执，造成大约300名拉科塔人被屠杀了，其中有一半人是妇女和儿童。联邦军中也有25人死亡了。事后，这起屠杀事件被确认为"战役"，而联邦政府将20枚荣誉勋章——即美国军队中最高级别的奖章——颁发给了联邦军队里的将士。这真可以说是光天化日下"掩耳盗铃"的例证，因为任何一个客观的旁观者都知道这是一起大屠杀。1965年，该屠杀场地被认定为国家历史文物保护点。1990年，在大屠杀发生百年之际，国会通过了一项决议，正式表达了对此一事件"深切的遗憾"。2019年，参议员伊丽莎白·沃伦预备提出一项议案，建议收回当时颁发给联邦军将士的那20枚荣誉勋章。

Vocabulary

103.	伤膝溪	**Shāngxī Xī**	Wounded Knee Creek
104.	屠杀	**túshā**	slaughter, massacre
105.	普遍	**pǔbiàn**	commonly
106.	臭名昭著	**chòumíng zhāozhù**	notorious
107.	惨案	**cǎn'àn**	massacre, tragedy
108.	终于	**zhōngyú**	finally
109.	承认	**chéngrèn**	to admit
110.	扩张	**kuòzhāng**	to expand
111.	开拓	**kāituò**	to pioneer
112.	原住民	**yuánzhùmín**	indigenous people
113.	正面	**zhèngmiàn**	directly
114.	被迫	**bèipò**	to be forced to
115.	居住地	**jūzhùdì**	home territory, land of one's home
116.	退让	**tuìràng**	to yield
117.	联邦	**liánbāng**	federal
118.	涉及	**shèjí**	to involve
119.	拉科塔部落	**Lākētǎ bùluò**	the Lakota tribe
120.	南达科塔州	**Nán Dákētǎ zhōu**	South Dakota
121.	拉科塔松岭印第安人保留区	**Lākētǎ Sōnglǐng Yìndì'ānrén Bǎoliúqū**	Lakota Pine Ridge Indian Reservation
122.	包围	**bāowéi**	to surround
123.	武器	**wǔqì**	weapons
124.	误会	**wùhuì**	misunderstanding
125.	引发	**yǐnfā**	to trigger
126.	争执	**zhēngzhí**	a dispute, a clash
127.	确认	**quèrèn**	to affirm, to acknowledge
128.	战役	**zhànyì**	battle
129.	荣誉勋章	**róngyù xūnzhāng**	medal of honor
130.	奖章	**jiǎngzhāng**	medal

131.	颁发	bānfā	to issue (an award, a diploma, etc.)
132.	光天化日	guāngtiān huàrì	in broad daylight
133.	例证	lìzhèng	example, proof
134.	任何	rènhé	any
135.	客观	kèguān	objective
136.	旁观者	pángguānzhě	bystander
137.	该	gāi	the said ..., the ... in question (formal)
138.	认定	rèndìng	to recognize as, to be designated
139.	文物保护点	wénwù bǎohùdiǎn	historic landmark (lit. "historical object protected site")
140.	…之际	...zhījì	at the time of ...
141.	国会	guóhuì	Congress
142.	决议	juéyì	resolution
143.	深切的遗憾	shēnqiède yíhàn	deep regret
144.	参议员	cányìyuán	senator
145.	议案	yì'àn	proposal, a motion

Discussion questions (discuss in English or Chinese):

1. Can you think of anyone you know whom you can describe as having "covered his ears while stealing a bell"?

2. No one is perfect. Can you think of an instance where someone pointed out one of your failings to you? How did you react to the critique, and how has the incident changed you?

3. Knowing that most people do not take criticism well, how would you help your friends see their personality flaws so that they may improve?

The Underdog Who Changed History

This is another true story from the Three Kingdoms period, about the legendary hero Lü Meng (178–220 CE),* who started life fatherless and poor, living in the household of his sister and brother-in-law, an army commander. Lü Meng was rough and uneducated but fearless—some might say foolhardy. At the age of fourteen, he stealthily joined his brother-in-law's army unit. Although Lü Meng was discovered, his family could not deter him. Because he was young and uncouth, however, he was poorly treated in the army. One commander said of him: "What can this kid do? He will end up feeding himself to the tigers." Enraged by this, Lü Meng drew his sword and killed the commander with a single blow. For this, he should have been executed. But the general in charge saw the heroic side of his personality and appointed Lü Meng to be his personal aide instead. This was Lü Meng's first lucky break!

---

* For a summary of the Three Kingdoms period, see the first two paragraphs of Chapter 14 "Planning Lies with Man But Success Lies with Heaven"

士别三日，刮目相看

这篇故事的<u>主人公</u>是三国时期的另一位<u>传奇</u>英雄吕蒙 (178–220)。* 吕蒙<u>出生低微</u>，家境贫困，又因为从小就失去了父亲，只好跟着在军中担任<u>将领</u>的姐夫。少年吕蒙没读过书，<u>勇猛鲁莽</u>。十四岁那年，吕蒙偷偷地跟随姐夫的军队外出<u>作战</u>。家人发现以后，谁也拦不住他的<u>牛脾气</u>。在军队里，大家也都看不上年少又鲁莽的吕蒙。一名军中将领<u>嘲笑</u>他说："那<u>小子</u>有什么本事？将来只会拿自己<u>喂虎</u>！"吕蒙听了这话，<u>一怒之下</u>挥刀杀了那名将领。这件事情让大将军看到了吕蒙的<u>过人之处</u>，不但没有<u>处死</u>他，反而安排他做了身边的<u>随从</u>！可以说是<u>幸运之神</u>第一次<u>眷顾</u>了吕蒙。

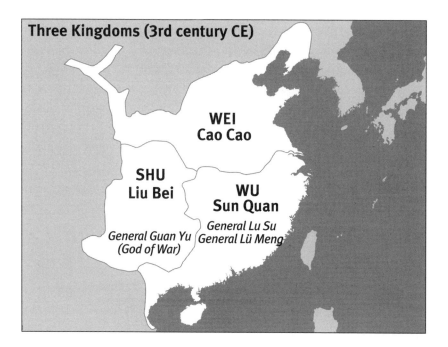

---

* 有关三国时期的简介，见本书第十四章"谋事在人，成事在天"的前两段。

Aside from being fearless, Lü Meng was also smart and persistent. He got another lucky break when the warlord Sun Quan (later to become the ruler of the Kingdom of Wu) exhorted him to read military history books. Lü Meng demurred, giving the excuse that his hands were full with his military duties. But Sun Quan cited the examples of many notable heroes past and present who had excelled through self-study. This set Lü Meng on a path of learning and laid the foundation for his future success.

At this time, the Eastern Han dynasty (25–220 CE) was in decline. The country was partitioned into three regions controlled by warlords fighting each other for hegemony: Cao Cao in the north, Liu Bei in the southwest and Sun Quan in the southeast (see map on page 243). The province of Jing—straddling present day Hunan, Hubei and Henan—was the central battleground. At first, the two southern warlords were allied against Cao Cao in the north. Both southern allies had brilliant commanders—General Guan Yu under Liu Bei and General Lu Su under Sun Quan.

A chance encounter with General Lu Su brought Lü Meng his next lucky break. Lu Su had always regarded Lü Meng as an ignorant and coarse person, calling him "The *Ah Meng* from the House of Wu." One day, as he was completing a round of inspections, Lu Su was passing Lü Meng's encampment but thought it wasn't worth a stop. However an aide informed him of Lü Meng's rapidly rising reputation, so Lu Su changed his mind and decided to drop in. Lü Meng greeted Lu Su with great ceremony and staged an elaborate banquet. While wining and dining him, Lü Meng warned Lu Su that their current ally, General Guan Yu, could turn into a rival and become their greatest enemy. He proposed five stratagems to deal with the formidable Guan Yu. Lu Su was amazed at Lü Meng's insights and ingenuity, whereupon he remarked with a deep bow, "Oh my, sir, you have totally changed and are no longer 'The *Ah Meng* from the House of Wu'!" To this, Lü Meng replied: "When a man of learning has been away for three days, you should view him with a fresh pair of eyes."

From that point on, Lü Meng became one of Sun Quan's leading generals. Upon Lu Su's death in 217 CE, Lü Meng succeeded him as the commander of Sun Quan's army. Like other legendary heroes of the Three Kingdoms era, his military triumphs on the battlefield came not from superior force but from cunning and ingenuity. He was a master of deception, luring his opponents into traps from which they could not escape.

除了勇猛过人以外，吕蒙还很聪明又很有毅力。当孙权（后来成为了三国中的一国之君）规劝吕蒙学习一些军事历史典籍的时候，吕蒙起初推脱军务繁忙，没空读书。孙权循循劝导，一一列举了历史上通过自学成就伟业的英雄们，吕蒙从此开悟，发奋读书，为日后功成名就打下了基础。

与此同时，东汉（25–220）政权日渐衰弱，而北魏的曹操，西蜀的刘备和东吴的孙权正形成三权争霸的局面。三军争夺的军事要地之一就是历史上的荆州，也就是今天湖南、湖北和河南的一大片土地。当时，蜀吴两军结成联盟，共同抵御曹操，而两军中都有足智多谋又骁勇善战的军事奇才，包括刘备手下的大将军关羽和孙权军中的大统领鲁肃。

吕蒙与大统领鲁肃的一次会面给他带来了晋升的契机。鲁肃一向以为吕蒙鲁莽无知而看不起他，当他是"吴下阿蒙。"有一天，鲁肃察看军情，路过吕蒙的营地，就打算绕过去。然而，身边的随从劝说鲁肃："吕将军在军中的威望越来越高，您应该进去拜访他。"鲁肃想，那就进去打个招呼吧。在营地里，吕蒙设宴款待了鲁肃。交谈间，吕蒙告诫鲁肃眼下的蜀吴联盟将来可能反目成仇，而关羽就将成为东吴最大的威胁，并给鲁肃建议了对付关羽的五大计策。看着侃侃而谈的吕蒙，鲁肃惊讶得下巴都快掉下来了，连连说道："佩服，佩服，吕将军真是脱胎换骨，已不再是'吴下阿蒙'了！"听了这话，吕蒙笑着回答："士别三日，当刮目相看嘛！"

此后，吕蒙成为了孙权军中最优秀的大将军之一。在鲁肃病故之后，吕蒙于公元217年接替鲁肃，晋升为孙权军中的最高统领。正如三国时期其他一些传奇英雄一样，吕蒙在军事上的成功并非因为他魁梧强壮，而是由于他足智多谋，懂得如何诱敌深入，落进他设下的圈套。

Lü Meng's final battle was against the great General Guan Yu. In Chinese culture, Guan Yu has been deified as the God of War and he was indeed a formidable foe. At this time, Lü Meng was seriously ill, but he used his illness to create a ruse, pretending to return home to seek medical treatment, thus luring Guan Yu's troops to vacate a strategic city. At the same time, he clandestinely repositioned his own troops to attack the unguarded city moat. This battle brought a quick and final victory to Lü Meng. Guan Yu and his son were captured and subsequently executed. Sadly, Lü Meng also died from his illness shortly after this victory, at the age of only 42.

Sometimes a single individual can change the course of history, especially in times of chaos. One might argue that Lü Meng's final victory was a turning point, for it strengthened Sun Quan's power so that the state of Wu became the third leg in a tripartite division of China for the next 43 years (220–263 CE). Without Lü Meng, there might not have been the Three Kingdoms as we know them today. Moreover, his life exemplifies the transformative power of education—in his case, self-study. For this, he is immortalized by the proverb: "When a man of learning has been away for three days, he must be viewed with a fresh pair of eyes."

The Chinese Proverb

士	别	三	日,	刮	目	相	看
shì	bié	sān	rì,	guā	mù	xiāng	kàn
a scholar	to part	three	days,	to scrape	eyes	toward (another), each other	to look

Literal meaning: When a person of learning has been away for three days, people should "scrape their eyes" when they look at him again.

Connotation: When a man of learning has been away for even a short time, one should look at him with a fresh pair of eyes. This proverb is applied to people who can make great progress within a short time.

The original source: Records of the Three Kingdoms, biography of Lü Meng in the Chapter on the State of Wu. Compiled by Chen Shou (233–297) during the Western Jin Dynasty. 《三国志•吴志•吕蒙传》西晋•陈寿 (233–297)著

吕蒙的最后一战就是在荆州与关羽之间的<u>较量</u>。在中国文化中，关羽被<u>尊</u>为"<u>武圣</u>，"可见他是一个多么厉害的<u>敌手</u>。这时，吕蒙已病重，然而在荆州之战中，他<u>假借</u>回江东就<u>医</u>设下了圈套，以<u>诱骗</u>关羽部队出城，并<u>暗中</u>调动军队，<u>攻击</u>了关羽没有<u>防守</u>的城池。吕蒙在这次战役中大获全胜，而关羽父子都被<u>抓获</u>，随后被处死了。可惜在这次胜利之后不久，吕蒙就病故了，去世时年仅42岁。

　　有时候，一个人的力量就可以改变历史的<u>进程</u>，尤其是在<u>乱世</u>时期。可以说吕蒙最后一战的胜利<u>巩固</u>了孙权的<u>势力</u>，<u>奠定</u>了东吴形成三国<u>鼎立</u>的局面，并维持了长达43年的政权（220－263）。没有吕蒙，可能就没有我们今天<u>熟知</u>的三国。吕蒙的<u>生平诠释</u>了教育改变<u>命运</u>的巨大作用。因此，他成为了自我教育<u>成才</u>的<u>典范</u>，而　"士别三日，刮目相看"也成为了中国的<u>经典谚语</u>。

Vocabulary

1.	士别三日， 刮目相看	**shì bié sān rì, guā mù xiāng kàn**	(see explanation in "The Chinese Proverb" section)
2.	主人公	**zhǔréngōng**	main character (in a story or play)
3.	传奇	**chuánqí**	legendary
4.	低微	**dīwēi**	lowly
5.	贫困	**pínkùn**	impoverished
6.	担任	**dānrèn**	to serve in the capacity of
7.	将领	**jiànglǐng**	military leader
8.	勇猛鲁莽	**yǒngměng lǔmǎng**	bold and reckless
9.	偷偷地	**tōutōude**	surreptitiously
10.	作战	**zuòzhàn**	to fight in battle
11.	拦不住	**lánbuzhù**	unable to restrain (someone) from ...

12.	牛脾气	niúpíqi	stubbornness (lit. "temperament of an ox")
13.	年少	niánshào	young of age
14.	嘲笑	cháoxiào	to make fun of (someone)
15.	小子	xiǎozi	little guy (derogatory)
16.	喂	wèi	to feed
17.	一怒之下	yínù zhī xià	in a rage
18.	挥刀	huī dāo	to brandish the sword
19.	将军	jiāngjun	military general
20.	过人之处	guò rén zhī chù	outstanding trait
21.	处死	chǔsǐ	to execute, to put to death
22.	随从	suícóng	entourage, retinue
23.	幸运之神	xìngyùn zhī shen	the god of luck
24.	眷顾	juàngù	to bestow grace on (someone)
25.	毅力	yìlì	perseverance
26.	君	jūn	king, ruler
27.	规劝	guīquàn	to admonish
28.	典籍	diǎnjí	classical books
29.	推脱	tuītuō	to beg off with an excuse
30.	繁忙	fánmáng	busy, occupied (with work)
31.	循循劝导	xúnxún quàndǎo	to methodically admonish or persuade
32.	列举	lièjǔ	to enumerate, to cite one by one
33.	成就伟业	chéngjiù wěiyè	to achieve great accomplishments
34.	开悟	kāiwù	to become enlightened
35.	发奋	fāfèn	to make a determined effort
36.	功成名就	gōngchéng míngjiù	to achieve success and fame
37.	与此同时	yǔ cǐ tóngshí	at the same time as this, meanwhile
38.	政权	zhèngquán	political power, regime
39.	日渐	rìjiàn	gradually, day by day
40.	衰弱	shuāiruò	to decline, to become weak

41.	三权争霸	sānquán zhēngbà	the three powers contending for supremacy
42.	局面	júmiàn	situation, state of affairs
43.	争夺	zhēngduó	to fight over
44.	要地	yàodì	key territory
45.	联盟	liánméng	alliance
46.	抵御	dǐyù	to resist
47.	足智多谋	zúzhì-duōmóu	wise and full of stratagems
48.	骁勇善战	xiāoyǒng shànzhan	brave and skilled in battle
49.	奇才	qícái	genius, extraordinary talent
50.	统领	tǒnglǐng	commander-in-chief
51.	晋升	jìnshēng	to be promoted to higher office
52.	契机	qìjī	turning point
53.	吴下阿蒙	Wú xià Ā Méng	"Little" Meng under the house of Wu
54.	察看	chákàn	to inspect
55.	营地	yíngdì	encampment
56.	绕过去	rào-guòqu	to skirt around
57.	威望	wēiwàng	prestige
58.	拜访	bàifǎng	to pay a visit (respectful)
59.	打⋯招呼	dǎ...zhāohu	to say hello, to pay a visit
60.	设宴	shèyàn	to put on a banquet
61.	款待	kuǎndài	to treat royally
62.	告诫	gàojiè	to warn
63.	眼下	yǎnxià	at present
64.	反目成仇	fǎn mù chéng chóu	(of friends or allies) turn against each other
65.	威胁	wēixié	threat; to threaten
66.	对付	duìfu	to counter, to deal with
67.	计策	jìcè	stratagem
68.	侃侃而谈	kǎnkǎn ér tán	to talk with ease and confidence
69.	惊讶	jīngyà	surprised

70.	下巴	**xiàba**	lower jaw, chin
71.	佩服	**pèifu**	to admire, to hold in high esteem
72.	脱胎换骨	**tuōtāi huàngǔ**	to be reborn, to be totally remolded
73.	病故	**bìnggù**	to die of illness
74.	接替	**jiētì**	to take over (a position)
75.	魁梧强壮	**kuíwú qiángzhuàng**	well-built and strong
76.	诱敌深入	**yòudí shēnrù**	to lure the enemy into a deep trap
77.	设下⋯圈套	**shèxià...quāntào**	to set a trap
78.	较量	**jiàoliàng**	to engage in a contest of strength
79.	尊	**zūn**	to respect, to honor
80.	武圣	**wǔ shèng**	God of War
81.	敌手	**díshǒu**	enemy, rival
82.	假借	**jiǎjiè**	to make use of a pretense
83.	就医	**jiùyī**	to seek medical treatment
84.	诱骗	**yòupiàn**	to lure by trickery
85.	暗中	**ànzhōng**	furtively, clandestinely
86.	调动	**diàodòng**	to transfer, to move (troops)
87.	攻击	**gōngjī**	to attack
88.	防守	**fángshǒu**	to defend, to guard
89.	城池	**chéngchí**	city moat
90.	战役	**zhànyì**	campaign, battle
91.	抓获	**zhuāhuò**	to capture
92.	进程	**jìnchéng**	process, progression, course
93.	乱世	**luànshì**	turbulent times
94.	巩固	**gǒnggù**	to consolidate, to establish firmly
95.	势力	**shìlì**	power

96.	奠定	**diàndìng**	to establish, to lay the foundation
97.	鼎立	**dǐnglì**	to stand like the three legs of a tripod
98.	维持	**wéichí**	to maintain
99.	熟知	**shúzhī**	to know very well
100.	生平	**shēngpíng**	all one's life
101.	诠释	**quánshì**	to annotate, to explain, to exemplify
102.	命运	**mìngyùn**	destiny
103.	成才	**chéngcái**	to become an accomplished person
104.	典范	**diǎnfàn**	model
105.	经典	**jīngdiǎn**	classic
106.	谚语	**yànyǔ**	proverb, adage

A Life Transformed by Education

Near the end of the 20th century, another Lü Meng was born in the hinterlands of China. Chinese parents tend to indulge in wishful thinking in naming their children. Even before Lü Meng was born, her parents had visions of their child inheriting the spirit of the legendary Lü Meng, and it didn't matter that their child turned out to be a girl.

Like many children growing up in rural China, Lü Meng was left behind to be raised by her grandmother while her parents migrated to a big city to make a living. With no access to China's best educational opportunities, her future looked unpromising. By chance, her family met an American professor who couldn't bear to see the vast amount of young talent in China going to waste for lack of education. Lü Meng, with her guileless charm, somehow inspired this professor to help her realize her potential. On her fifteenth birthday, the first day that she could legally fly on an American airline unaccompanied, she flew to the other side of the world to begin her education with the support of this professor. Twelve years later, when she completed her doctorate in psychology, she revisited her hometown, where she was greeted with various versions of "Oh my, Lü Meng is no longer one of those 'left-behind children' of rural China!" To which Lü Meng murmured, "When a person of learning has been away for a few years, she must be viewed with a fresh pair of eyes!"

This story is totally true. The American professor in the story is one of the co-authors of this book!

教育改变了她的命运

在二十世纪末年，另一位吕蒙在中国的东北出生了。中国父母在给孩子起名时往往寄予厚望。在吕蒙将要出生之时，她父母就已经希望孩子能继承传奇英雄吕蒙的基因，即使生下女孩儿也没关系。

　　吕蒙很小的时候，她父母就去了北京谋生，而吕蒙就像许许多多生长在中国农村地区的孩子一样，成了一名留守儿童，留在家乡让姥姥带大。因为没有机会享受良好的教育，吕蒙的前途一片茫然。很偶然的机会，吕蒙的父母在城里认识了一位美国教授，而这位教授实在不忍心看着大批的中国孩子因为缺乏受教育的机会而荒废了学业。淳朴憨厚的小吕蒙打动了这位教授，愿意助她一臂之力来发掘还未可知的潜力。在吕蒙十五岁生日的那天，也就是她可以合法地在没有大人的陪伴下乘坐美国航空公司飞机的第一天，吕蒙飞越了太平洋，抵达了世界的另一端，开始了在这位教授支助下的求学生涯。十二年后，吕蒙取得了心理学博士学位。当她重访老家时，亲友们都报以各种惊叹："天哪，吕蒙不再是那个小留守儿童了！"听到这些话，吕蒙总是喃喃地说："士别三日，当刮目相看啊！"

　　本事例为真实故事。文中的美国教授是本书作者之一！

Vocabulary

107.	命运	**mìngyùn**	destiny, fate
108.	末年	**mònián**	final years (of an era)
109.	寄予厚望	**jìyǔ hòuwàng**	to place high hopes
110.	继承	**jìchéng**	to inherit, to become heir to
111.	基因	**jīyīn**	genes
112.	谋生	**móushēng**	to make a living
113.	留守儿童	**liúshǒu értóng**	"left-behind children"
114.	前途	**qiántú**	future prospects
115.	茫然	**mángrán**	at a loss; indistinct
116.	偶然	**ǒurán**	by chance, fortuitously
117.	不忍心	**bù rěnxīn**	cannot bear to...
118.	荒废	**huāngfèi**	to lie wasted; uncultivated
119.	淳朴憨厚	**chúnpǔ hānhou**	guileless and down-to-earth
120.	打动	**dǎdòng**	to touch (someone emotionally)
121.	助···一臂之力	**zhù...yíbì zhī lì**	to lend a helping hand
122.	发掘	**fājué**	to unearth, to develop
123.	未可知	**wèi kě zhī**	not yet knowable, still unknown
124.	潜力	**qiánlì**	potential
125.	合法	**héfǎ**	legal
126.	陪伴	**péibàn**	to accompany
127.	航空	**hángkōng**	aviation
128.	飞越	**fēiyuè**	to fly over (a wide expanse)
129.	太平洋	**Tàipíngyáng**	Pacific Ocean
130.	抵达	**dǐdá**	to reach (a destination)
131.	端	**duān**	end, point
132.	支助	**zhīzhù**	to support; support
133.	求学	**qiúxué**	to seek learning, to get an education

134. 生涯	shēngyá	career
135. 心理学	xīnlǐxué	psychology
136. 重访	chóngfǎng	to revisit
137. 报以	bàoyǐ	to give in return, to respond with
138. 惊叹	jīngtàn	to exclaim in wonderment
139. 喃喃地	nánnánde	to murmur, to mumble
140. 事例	shìlì	instance, occurrence

Discussion questions (discuss in English or Chinese):

1. Have you ever witnessed a surprising transformation in a person whom you haven't seen in a while that befits the proverb introduced in this chapter?

2. The story tells of Lü Meng's two lucky breaks. Was he just lucky, or did those two superiors see something in Lü Meng that merited special consideration?

3. The Chinese have another saying: 好男不当兵、好铁不打钉 **hǎo nán bù dāng bīng, hǎo tiě bù dǎ dīng** "Good men do not become soldiers; good iron is not hammered into nails." How do you think this attitude squares with the worship of military heroes in Chinese culture?

About the Authors

Vivian Ling was a professor of Chinese language and literature for over four decades. She has taught at Oberlin College and Indiana University, and has directed various Chinese language study-abroad programs in Taipei, Shanghai, Kunming and Beijing. She is the author of several Chinese language textbooks and books on related subjects, including *The Field of Chinese Language Education in the U.S.: A Retrospective of the 20th Century*.

Wang Peng has been on the faculty at Georgetown University since 2002, teaching various Chinese language courses including Business Chinese and Chinese for Heritage Learners. Formerly, she was the chief instructor at the Inter-University Program for Chinese Language Studies at Tsinghua University, as well as visiting faculty at Oberlin College and Brown University.

About the Illustrator

Yang Xi 杨熙 is an up-and-coming artist and illustrator in China. Her distinctive style can be characterized as an amalgamation of classical and contemporary, Chinese and Western. She is currently a Master of Arts candidate at the Nanjing Art Institute College of Fine Arts. Her contribution to this book of Chinese proverbs and folktales is her debut in a publication outside of China.